# Fashion sewing

# by the

# Bishop method

**Edna Bryte Bishop**

*Originator and Developer of the Bishop Method*

**Marjorie Stotler Arch**

*Associate Educational Director, Advance Pattern Company*

*Pattern Sketches by* Dorothy L. Davids
*Line drawings for Chapters*
*1 and 2 by* Anna R. Atene

*Photographs by* Stewart Love

**J. B. Lippincott Company** *Philadelphia • New York*

# CONTENTS

Library of Congress Catalog No.: 62–16378

Copyright © 1962
by J. B. Lippincott Company

*Printed in the United States of America*

# PREFACE

This new book, *Fashion Sewing by the Bishop Method,* is designed to help everyone who sews achieve the quality look in all home sewing. The homemaker who sews to find a creative outlet, or who sews to stretch the family budget, now can be sure of doing a professional-looking job by learning the principles of The Bishop Method and by applying them to everyday clothing problems.

The authors' first book, *The Bishop Method of Clothing Construction,* set forth the following fundamental principles of clothing construction: grain perfection; accuracy in preparing, cutting, and marking fabric; cutting to fit; perfection in stitching; perfection in pressing; and correct trimming detail. These basic principles were developed in detail to enable all who used the first Bishop-Arch book to improve their standards of sewing workmanship.

In this second book by the same authors, *Fashion Sewing by the Bishop Method,* the construction principles of the first book are used as the foundation for improving the specific techniques and special skills essential in dealing with the many and varied sewing problems related to clothing all members of the family. A study of the Table of Contents will reveal the challenging nature and the broad scope of the sewing projects covered.

This new book is not a revision of, nor a replacement for, the first book. There is a real need for both books. You must have the first one to master thoroughly the basic learnings, which, incidentally, are not repeated in this book. You will want the second one to extend these basic learnings and to apply them successfully in the development and improvement of your own sewing techniques.

The important part that sewing plays in modern living calls for a new type of book, one which will meet present-day sewing needs and standards. The girl or woman who sews today has good taste, wants to choose her own pattern and fabric, insists on a style closely identified with her personality, and will settle for nothing less smart than the blouse, dress, or suit which she sees in the best shops. *Fashion Sewing by the Bishop Method* will help every girl and woman attain her individual sewing goals.

In using the book, even though you may not follow through in making all of the garments in any given chapter, you should study the entire chapter to learn all the principles of the Bishop method involved in making garments of each particular type.

In schools, the book can be used from junior high-school level all the way through college level. The chapters used must be chosen to meet the needs, interests, and abilities of the group.

We especially want to give credit and to express our sincere thanks to J. L. Hudson Co. of Detroit, and to Royers in Greensburg, Pennsylvania, for their cooperation with the chapter on alterations of ready-to-wear. Our thanks, also, are extended to Dorothy Davids, artist, and Stewart Love, photographer, for their untiring efforts in helping us to complete the book, and to Joseph Horne Co. of Pittsburgh.

Whether you approach sewing as an art or as a necessity, we present this second book in the hope that you will receive as much enjoyment in using it as we did in writing it for you.

*Edna Bryte Bishop*
*Marjorie Stotler Arch*

# Chapter 1

# The well-dressed woman

Being well dressed is one of the finest arts in the world, and there are many things to know and learn in developing this art in ourselves. After you have studied the two chapters on dressing smartly, perhaps you will be able to develop a working plan by listing the *no's* and *must's* that apply to *you*.

### Developing the art of being well dressed

You should begin by learning the difference between good and bad taste. Good taste in dress is not a question of money but rather a question of knowledge. What is good taste? It is an expression of personal style to suit your own physical proportions, your personality, and your way of life. It is the ability to judge what is beautiful, appropriate, and harmonious for you. You must learn to distinguish real beauty and elegance from the tricky or eye-catching fashion so frequently seen around us. You may often have to determine your purchases quite apart from personal preference, and test them by the same criteria you would use in viewing a painting or a work of sculpture. Fashion is truly a visual proof of taste.

Then, if taste is what you choose, style is how you wear it. Together, they make elegance in *you*. No amount of wealth can buy style. It takes self-respect, self-discipline, and a good sense of values. Some people have said that style results more from the way one's clothes are worn than from the clothes themselves. It is an elegance which reflects individual personality and vitality. These things are important because your appearance is the way you present yourself to the world.

### Here are some points to remember:

1. People with good taste realize the importance of wearing the appropriate clothes for the right occasion. Perhaps, you should begin by analyzing how many sides there are to your life around which to plan your clothes—home, business, sports, social life, travel, and many others.

4. Clothes that are right for you last through the years. Be careful about buying *extreme* fashions, especially in large or expensive items. These may last only one season. A good coat should last five years.

5. Aim to develop a first rate *you*; if fashion seems to be dictating anything that isn't right for you, ignore it. We say that discipline in clothes is a clearcut picture of your own identity as a person. Use fashion instead of fashion using you.

6. Build your wardrobe around never-out-of-season clothes, known as classics.

7. An approach toward complete costume planning is the dress and jacket concept—informal with the jacket on, formal with the jacket off. This will, of course, depend upon the style and fabric from which they are made.

2. Next, before buying anything, review your wardrobe, discarding items you are not likely to wear again. Make a careful wardrobe plan and never, as you shop, depart from your plan by buying a tempting "pretty" that you might or might not ever wear. Choose things that *go together*. Determine one or two basic colors around which your wardrobe will be built, together with two or three colors for accessories, shoes, hats, and gloves. Remember that a man's point of view about clothes is concerned with how pleasing a picture you will make; he will look at the whole ensemble rather than at its separate parts.

You might ask yourself these questions before you make a purchase:

> How will it wear?
> Will it keep its shape?
> Will it become dated?
> Where will it take me?
> How does it fit into my life?

3. Garments such as coats, suits, and dresses, which are worn longest and are most expensive, should be purchased first, then used as a nucleus around which other wardrobe needs are harmonized.

8. The word "functional" has dictated much in American fashion; but too often, it has been interpreted to mean casual, and casual often becomes *too casual*. One example is the number of tourists who visit our nation's capital in shorts and slacks. Complement a public building by your choice of clothes, for you have already learned that your appearance is the way you present yourself to the world. It is not alone just what you wear, but where you wear it.

9. Do not appear on city streets in flat shoes, head scarfs, huge skirts, strapless dresses, or with your hair in pin curls.

10. Ladylike may be the nicest adjective you can merit.

11. The style, color, and fabric in a costume must be exactly right for you. You will learn much about them in these two chapters. Then, just as they play an important role, so do fit and workmanship, because inferior workmanship and poor fit can never be concealed.

12. Do not ever hesitate to wear a becoming costume many, many times.

13. You should have just *one* outstanding or important thing in a costume at a time, such as a beautiful needlepoint bag, a lovely embroidered jacket, or a distinctive hat. Yet, every costume you wear should have something intriguing about it. Judge how you will look twenty feet away!

14. There should never be more than one focal point to a costume. If you wear a brightly colored coat, you must wear a black dress.

15. Many women realize the importance of having something to draw attention to them.

16. Remember that too many spots of contrast are never good in a costume. You must not look cluttered, faddish, or disorganized. For example, on some people, the contrast in a costume is better in the hat and jewelry or collar to form a framework for the face. White gloves moving around a dark costume detract from the face.

17. Check for balance in your costume; for example, the hat which may have a large flower on one side should never be worn when the dress is designed with a large drape on the same side.

18. Always dress yourself carefully, even at home, and remember that women were meant to be *feminine*. Comfortable clothes must never be careless clothes.

19. Now, the foundation has been laid for developing good taste and style to give elegance, charm, true chic, and distinction. These are worth striving for.

Let us analyze the separate parts of a costume.

## Choice of accessories

The right accessories can make a costume or ruin it, and they may cost more than your dress, suit, or coat. The most perfect dress, suit, or coat cannot stand on its own without the right wearer and the right accessories.

Accessories will change a costume, so it is wise to select some dresses, suits, and coats you can dress up *or* dress down. Consider a gold pin versus a rhinestone one, a black jersey sash versus a black satin one, and a large leather bag versus a small satin clutch bag.

Accessories must be appropriate. Never wear fancy shoes with a sports costume, long, dangle earrings for traveling, or a business-like leather or straw bag with a filmy frock.

Also, have only one outstanding or important thing in a costume at a time, such as a hat with brightly colored flowers, a plaid suit, or a leopard muff. Yet, every costume you wear should have something intriguing about it.

Don't wear *everything* at once. It is a great American fault. We refer you to the all-important point system for dressing smartly on page 192, *The Bishop Method of Clothing Construction*.

It may take some time to build up a wardrobe of the right accessories, but good leather bags, gloves, and shoes are marks of a well-dressed person.

**Hats.** 1. A hat is usually the most important accessory to a smart appearance. It lifts an individual into another status and is a symbol of a woman.

2. Did you ever see a suit in a display window without a hat? The suit or the ensemble is incomplete without the right hat.

3. A hat should be ladylike, with great dignity and charm.

4. Develop a flair for wearing hats smartly.

5. Do not buy nondescript millinery. Make every hat tell a story, fit an ensemble, fill a fashion need. It should have distinction twenty feet away.

6. Yet, the fancier a costume is, the simpler the hat must be.

7. It is much better to buy a hat to go with one or two garments than to try to have one hat go with everything.

8. A hat is the frame for your face.

9. A hat must be in the right relationship for your face, head, and style of costume. Study the relationship to your face, head, and hair style, not only from the front but from the side and back.

10. Even the most perfect figure would look awkward in a wide hat combined with a boxy jacket and a wide skirt.

11.  A short, heavy figure looks even shorter and becomes top-heavy under a large, wide hat.

12.  If your shoulders are extremely wide and your face is full, a hat should not extend in width beyond the middle of your shoulders.

13.  Never buy a hat until you have had a look at yourself in a full-length mirror.

14.  When you are buying extreme fashion in a hat, particularly if it is very expensive, remember that you may only be able to wear it that one season.

15.  The hat made from matching fabric of coat or suit can lack smartness; too often a touch of the fireside is very apparent.  Too much sameness is seldom smart. If a matching fabric hat is your choice, make certain it enhances you and your costume.

16.  A hat should never be darker than your shoes.

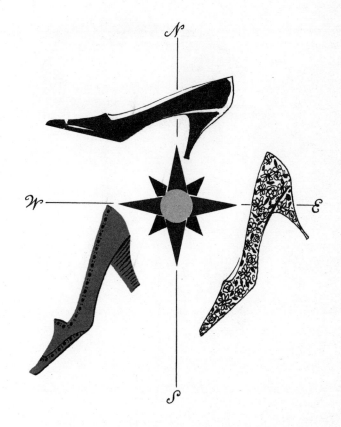

**Shoes.**  1.  The style of the shoe is most important in relation to the shape of the leg and ankle.  Pumps are universally our most flattering shoe style.

2.  Pumps are also our most universally accepted shoe style with most costumes.

3.  Select a height of heel that is flattering to your legs and ankles, and with which you can walk gracefully.  To be well dressed, you should wear heels.

4.  Don't wear bright-colored shoes or shoes with a fancy trim unless your feet are pretty.

5.  Heelless and toeless shoes are difficult to wear.

6.  Analyze the style of a shoe at the back in relation to your ankle.

7.  Of plastic shoes, we say that unless you consider feet to be pretty, why display them?  Occasionally, plastic slippers with an appropriate trim have been attractive for evening wear only.

8.  Don't spoil an evening ensemble with your go-with-everything black suede pumps!  Satin or silk shoes are a smarter choice.  Satin pumps in different colors (they may be dyed to match a dress or made a full tone deeper) are a classic addition for after-five clothes.

9.  If you choose patent leather pumps, don't wear them with sport clothes.

10.  Patent leather shoes can be worn almost the year around, depending upon your costume, and they are perfectly correct for informal, after-dark occasions.

11.  High-cut shoes and heavy ankle straps steal length from your legs.  Ankle straps make your ankles appear wider.

12.  White shoes belong only with a white or very light-colored costume.  They are never the correct groundwork for a dark costume.

13.  Nothing spoils an outfit more than timeworn shoes, and shoes which are obviously out of style.

14.  Shoes covered to match a costume (print shoes for a print dress for example) have proved to be a smart choice.  They may complement a costume more than any other shoes you can purchase.  However, you should not repeat the print *any other place.*

**Handbags.**  1.  Select a size of handbag in relation to the number of articles you like to carry in one, so that it can retain its shape.

2.  The size of a handbag should also be chosen in proportion to the height and size of the wearer. Hang it on your arm and analyze its size for you, or study yourself in a long mirror.

3.  If your gloves and bag match, and moreover if they match your costume, they will increase your height.

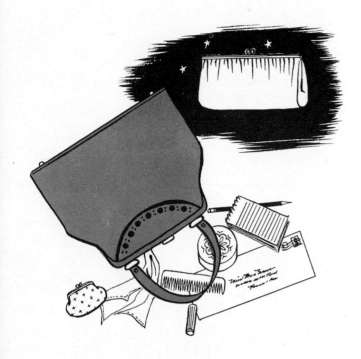

4. Anyone has a difficult time caring for a white bag.

5. Because you have a beautiful alligator bag, you needn't purchase alligator shoes to match. Ensembles are often overdone, and a beautiful alligator bag can very well stand on its own with leather pumps.

6. Huge leather carry-all or tote bags are wonderful for traveling or for shopping, but they should never be carried after five o'clock. When you leave home for a full day, you can put a small clutch bag in your tote bag.

7. Think twice about a bag that is decorated to look like a flower or fruit garden, or Sherwood Forest! One you can see through reveals everything you have inside, also!

8. A contrasting bag calls attention to your hips.

9. You will always look more graceful carrying a bag up on your arm at your waistline, instead of having it dangle at your side with your arm straight down.

**Gloves.** 1. Gloves are traditionally a sign of dignity, but not soiled ones! When wearing light-colored ones, always carry an extra pair in your purse.

2. There are informal occasions when gloves aren't needed, but always wear them on the street, even without a hat, to church, the theater, and luncheons.

3. Longer gloves are more dignified than short ones, although the length of gloves is partly controlled by the length of sleeves, by the attractiveness of your arms, and by the occasion to which they are being worn. Very formal occasions call for gloves extending up over the elbows.

4. Short, white gloves are smart with anything sleeveless or summery; or short black ones may be more interesting. Short, wrist-length gloves are often a smart choice for party dresses, also.

5. In some cases, no other accessory can do as much for a dress as the right pair of gloves.

6. Are white gloves always good? It is very often better to coordinate them with the colors in your outfit. Neutral shades are very popular.

7. If your forearms down to the wrist are overly heavy, avoid wrist-length gloves.

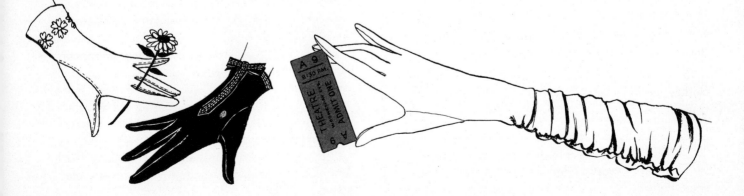

**Jewelry.** 1. Don't have everything match—those *sets* of earrings, bracelets, necklaces, etc!

2. Pearls are our most flattering jewelry and are correct at all times. Just be certain to get the right size for *you*, and the right length for the neckline of the dress.

3. Dare to be simple; if there are fancy buttons, let them be the focal point in your costume without other adornment. Don't obscure a beautiful neckline with a distracting necklace or beads.

4. Unless your pin expresses something about your costume, leave it in your dresser drawer, and look at it there! Wear pins imaginatively placed or paired—slipping out of a pocket or from under a lapel!

5. All pieces of jewelry worn at the same time should have some relationship to each other.

6. The rhinestone category in jewelry is still best after five, except that possibly a *small* rhinestone pin may be worn during the day.

7. Limit yourself on bracelets and rings if your hands aren't pretty, or they will reveal your age.

8. You should wear only one bracelet on plump arms, but you can wear many on long, thin arms.

9. The way your ears are formed will decide what kind of earrings you can wear.

10. If you have a round face, wear long pearls instead of chokers, or a pendant on a slim, long chain, and narrow, drop earrings instead of round or square ones.

11. If you have a long face, wear button or cluster earrings and a large choker high on the throat.

12. A thin neck is camouflaged with space-filling jewelry.

13. Buttons of a large ball variety add thickness to a thin figure.

14. If you are heavy, avoid glittery or eye-catching fastenings, large buttons, and massive pins.

15. A change of buttons or other trimmings on clothes you buy can make them more becoming and expensive looking.

16. Many women over 50 find silver jewelry more flattering than gold.

17. If you have an over-sized bust, avoid wearing too long or too bulky a necklace.

18. Avoid wearing too many pieces of jewelry at one time, such as a pin on a hat, earrings, necklace, lapel pin, watch, bracelets, and rings.

19. A touch of excitement can be added to a costume with the right jewelry: pearls, for example, with a strand or two of jade-green beads in their midst; emerald beads on a blue dress; or a huge turquoise pin on an herb-green dress.

**Miscellaneous things.** 1. Before selecting clothes, get the right foundation garments. You will need several styles for various styles in clothes. Try on a foundation before buying it, because all styles aren't for you.

2. You can wear too much underneath your clothes. A half-slip is better than a full slip in many cases.

3. Your slip should harmonize with the color of your costume. Lingerie is now available in many colors. Many people will sew a band of matching color of dress fabric around the lower edge of their slip. Always wear black lingerie with a black costume.

4. Do not go stockingless! Seams and long heels improve legs and ankles.

5. If your legs are ungainly, keep the color of your hose inconspicuous. However, darker hose are more flattering to legs than lighter ones. Remember that very dark hose look hot.

6. Many people who are all dressed up will pull bathroom tissue out of their handbag! You should always carry two handkerchiefs, and they should harmonize with your costume.

7. Many times for a dash of color or design, you can wear a scarf for a belt or hang one over your regular belt.

8. For the most part, best designers say that artificial flowers should be kept on hats! Exceptions are those made of self-fabric or lace.

9. A suit worn without a blouse, or with a blouse or little sweater the same or harmonizing color of the suit, gives the look of a complete ensemble. The little white blouse worn with every suit seldom gives the look of a complete, smart ensemble.

10. Short, stout people should wear short-haired, flat skins, such as broadtail and caracul; never bushy, bulky, or long-haired furs.

11. The style of a stole is as important as the style of your clothes. A full-length or medium deep stole with short ends is best on most people.

12. If a stole has long ends that come below the waistline, the individual must know how to wear it smartly.

13. A person who is short or wide should not wear a stole with long ends. Analyze the length of the back, also, for the size and height of the person. Neither a stole nor a jacket should cut a short person in half.

14. It is important that the cut and the shape of the collar, as well as the amount and the hang of the fullness of the stole, be right for the individual.

15. The color of the fur you choose should be just as flattering to your hair, skin, and eyes as any other color you choose for your costumes.

16. A little jacket or stole is often needed to cover that too bare look.

17. Thin, plastic raincoats are not a "well-dressed" choice.

18. Glasses should be a part of your personality, and not of your fashion wardrobe. Unless you have an extra, novelty pair for sportswear, the shape and color of the frames should blend with your facial tones and hair coloring.

19. If you wear glasses, especially if they have detail of trim in the frames, you *must* limit the amount of detail at your face in earrings, necklaces, and veiling or trims on a hat!

20. Select buttons under a good light. Use contrasting colored buttons with care so that they don't look spotty. When used, these buttons are generally the trimming detail of the dress; so keep the dress simple in design.

## Choice of color

Fortunately or unfortunately, color is our greatest accessory; it can destroy beauty as well as create it. Here are some tips on color to help you in developing the art of being well dressed.

1. No one should wear colors she does not like.

2. Give much thought to what a color will do for your figure, your skin, your hair, and your eyes.

3. You should think of color combined with texture, not of one or the other independently. Texture affects color—turquoise in satin versus jersey, red in soft velvet versus hard-finished taffeta, and brown in harsh gabardine versus soft fleece.

4. Take it easy on bright colors—a touch of gaiety will do a trick, but an avalanche will bury you.

5. Only those who are vivid in coloring should wear vivid colors in large areas. The less vivid the individual, the less apt she is to transcend strong color. People with soft coloring need more subdued color to enhance their own.

6. Sometimes, a little tint in the hair makes all the difference in the colors one can wear. It may only be a tint that is sprayed on the hair.

7. Lighter colors should lead to the top of the costume.

8. Remember that the eye always goes where contrast takes it.

9. Consider whether a color will soil easily or show lint, and how much care will be necessary to keep it looking fresh for the places it will be worn.

10. Never wear more than three outstanding colors in a costume at one time (unless a print shows more);

never use the same color more than three times. For example, a white hat and white jewelry would be desirable with a black dress, handbag, and shoes. Matching black gloves would be counted with the handbag. A bright hat, bag, shoes, gloves, and jacket would never be good; a bright hat and belt would be smarter.

This rule serves as a wonderful guide, but there can be exceptions to it; for example, some women can wear all black or all beige costumes smartly.

Then, the monochromatic color scheme is effective and popular in today's fashion. Shades from light blue to navy or from pale beige to dark brown are good examples of this approach.

11. Decide on basic colors in your costume planning; keep them firmly in mind, even if you are only shopping for handkerchiefs.

12. Fine fabrics cost money; color does not.

13. Overweight women will always look slimmer in colors medium to dark in tone. Dull black and subdued or grayed colors have a receding effect.

14. Since dark values of color tend to make a large figure recede, the opposite in light, warm colors should be used by the tall, thin figure.

15. Black has everything—dignity, elegance, sophistication, simplicity, chic.

16. Black and white are always considered dramatic together and can never be beaten as a color combination. Almost everyone can wear black and white. However, the aging, with graying hair and fading color, should beware of black, since it absorbs light and tends to drain light from the face.

17. Light, neutral hair is reduced to further drabness with beiges and tans.

18. Neutral colors, such as light beiges and grays, tend to be less interesting at night. Dominant colors, as well as black and white, are fine after dark.

19. Pink is considered a universally becoming color.

20. Turquoise is a good color for most women.

21. Deep pink and turquoise are good night and day colors.

22. Other delightful evening colors are gold and gray-blue.

23. Pale blue is a wonderful color.

24. Bravery never goes out of fashion in combining colors—electric blue with masses of white pearls, shades of blue with shades of green, brilliant plaid

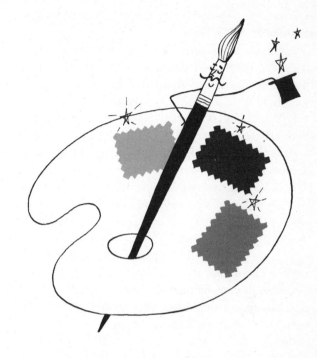

with chunky gold, or creamy salmon with turquoise jewelry.

25. Instead of thinking that you cannot wear a certain color, learn that you cannot wear certain shades of the color. You can wear almost any color if you find the right shade or value that is softened or grayed enough for you.

26. Do not wear two grayed colors at one time.

27. Some women can wear navy much better than black for a basic color in their wardrobe.

28. Always ask yourself what impression you wish your scheme to convey—vitality, drama, joy, dignity, maturity, or conservatism?

29. Lastly, the total effect of any color harmony depends not only on the colors chosen but also on the proportion in which each occurs and where they are placed with relation to each other.

COLOR IS PURE MAGIC!

### Necessary care of clothes for being well dressed

Here are some points to keep in mind:

1. Keep hemlines even; it is a full-time job, but very important.

2. Dress and skirt hems should be ½ inch shorter than full-length coats.

3. Your slip should never show. Always check in a full-length mirror.

4. Never hang up a garment wrong side out. Place it on a hanger grain perfect, fasten some of the buttons, and close zippers. Never leave belts on dress belt loops. Hang them separately.

5. Wire hangers are only meant to be carriers between the cleaner's and your home. Clothes must be supported by stronger hangers to hold their shape. Make certain skirts do not dip in the center with the style of skirt hanger you choose.

6. Do not wear limp veils, unpressed bows, or bent flowers on hats. Press hat veiling between two layers of wax paper to freshen it.

7. Your shoes should be polished or brushed, and the heels kept neat at all times. Don't forget to polish or brush your handbags, also.

8. Handbags should be pretty inside as well as out. Keep your compact fresh and clean, and replace the puff often.

9. Do not wear any garment that has a spot on it or is soiled in any way.

10. Discard old, limp gloves that you haven't worn in a year. Perfection in each pair of gloves is more important than the number of pairs you own.

11. Keep coats and other outer garments separate from lightweight clothes in closets, so they won't push them out of line.

12. If you wear a panty girdle, you can tuck your blouse inside it. This keeps your blouse in place with skirts or shorts.

13. Aside from carrying an extra handkerchief and pair of gloves in your handbag or tote bag, there will be occasions when you will want to carry an extra pair of stockings.

14. For perfection in grooming, clothes must be immaculately clean and pressed, with buttons, hooks, and snaps securely sewn in place, shoes well polished, heels neat, gloves well-fitting, and stockings never loose or twisted. Work toward a head-to-toe fastidiousness of grooming and dress.

15. To keep stocking seams perfectly straight, fasten your back supporter in the exact center of the seam at the full fashion mark (unless, of course, your girdle does not have a supporter placed at the back).

16. Never wear jewelry with missing stones.

17. Make-up and perfume will discolor some kinds of jewelry if you are not careful to prevent them from getting on it.

# Chapter 2

# The perfect dress, suit, or coat

### The lines of your costume

The lines of your costume produce movement, causing the eye to move in different directions—vertical, horizontal, and diagonal! Study every line of a pattern or dress in relation to your figure before you select it. Remember always that simple lines are best on everyone.

When studying the following rules about line, keep in mind that there will always be exceptions to every one of them.

**Lines of an entire ensemble.** 1. The favored standard figure is approximately 5 feet 6 inches tall. If you are taller, select lines to make you look shorter. If you are shorter, select lines to make you look taller. One of the most important factors of the ideal woman's figure is that the width of the shoulders and hips as measured across the front are the same.

2. Always wear a straight skirt with boxy garments that end below the waistline.

3. Never end a jacket or other garment at the widest part of large hips, or do anything else that will create a horizontal line there. Keep the jacket shorter or longer to form a pleasing proportion for the figure.

4. A semi-fitted jacket is recommended for the person with large hips and large bust. A jacket that is not fitted too close to the figure is younger and more becoming to most women.

5. If you are short and wish to look taller, jackets should match your skirt or dress, and short or long, keep them slim. A one-piece dress with a jacket is better than skirt, blouse, and jacket.

6. Double-breasted lines are good on the tall, slim figure, while single-breasted lines are better for the heavy or short figure.

7. If you or your daughter are chubby, do have vertical lines in your costume, and not horizontal lines. Upward slanting diagonals sometimes give added grace. Emphasis should always be within your silhouette.

8. If you are chubby, coats should be full length preferably, either straight or semi-fitted, with easy, long-fitting sleeves. The bulk of a big, loose coat with too much detail makes you appear larger.

9. A cardigan, chosen in the right length, is universally becoming with a straight skirt.

10. Many styles of dresses that button down the front make you look older and heavier.

11. A sheath dress does not look well on a heavy figure—a skirt with some fullness is more becoming.

12. It takes a tall, slim figure to wear a dress with a wide look in the cut of the bodice and in the cut of the skirt. Many figures can wear a wide look one place, but not both.

13. If you are short, wear slim, one-piece clothes; do not break the line with color or wide belts. Wide belts make you look squarer.

14. A ½-inch wide belt (narrow and inconspicuous, of self fabric) is more flattering to the figure with a

thick waist than a one-inch belt. Even a better choice may be to finish the waistline seam with a piece of bias (similar to middle photo, page 194, *The Bishop Method of Clothing Construction*), and eliminate a belt.

15. Contrast at the waistline is good for the tall, thin figure, since it will draw attention to this area and thereby cut the apparent height.

16. Much shirring on a garment makes the figure look heavier.

17. The tall, thin figure needs lines which attract the eye in a horizontal movement. She should avoid the clinging, too tight silhouette, and is best in the flattering effect of unpressed pleats, tucks, and other forms of flowing fullness. Boxy jackets are better than figure-revealing, fitted ones. In length, they may come to the hips, or any length below the hips which gives a pleasing proportion. Rarely are bolero jackets good for this figure, because they give the effect of too great length of limb.

18. Short shorts are for the teen-ager; bermuda shorts are more attractive on most women. Long pants are the kindest to figures with unattractive legs but good hips. In any length, slacks are flattering only to the women who have slim hips and a flat stomach.

19. Capes are good on the tall, thin person, since they tend to reduce height.

20. Do you enjoy the real pleasure of fashion to the extent that you can and will wear a coat smartly that has to be clutched all the time? All fashion requires the right wearer.

**The lines of the bodice.** 1. A strapless dress is a poor choice for the short person or one with thick shoulders or a large bust.

2. Wear sleeveless dresses only if your arms are slender, and never if you have overdeveloped arm muscles, any sign of flabbiness, or a heavy upper arm. Of course, you should not wear sleeveless dresses if your arms are too thin.

3. Dolman and raglan sleeves are good for square shoulders. They are not recommended for the figure that has narrow or sloping shoulders and large bust and hips. Set-in sleeves minimize the bust and hips.

4. Longer sleeves tend to camouflage the size of large forearms. The most flattering sleeve length is below the elbow.

5. Wide, loose sleeves tend to widen the figure.

6. Long, thin arms are concealed by the dolman or by wide, full sleeves with a band or deep cuff.

7. Consider carefully contrasting cuffs or puff sleeves; they make the figure look heavier and wider.

8. If the color of a sleeve is in sharp contrast to the color of your skin (black versus beige, for example), then the sleeve length is even more important to consider for your arm.

9. The all-in-one sleeve is simple to fit, almost universally becoming (see point 3), and can't be topped for comfort.

10. High round necklines are a focal spot for jewelry.

11. A square neckline fits better if it is slightly curved at the corners.

12. Necklines should be cut close at sides and back for a stout figure. The slightly lower neckline in front, such as a narrow square, will cut the thick look of shoulders and bust.

13. Collars for a heavy figure should be narrow and relatively flat. The shawl collar with a V neckline is one of the best. Outstanding lapels attract the eye and should be scaled to balance hip width.

14. The thin figure needs cover-up necklines, such as a cowl collar, scarfs, and soft bows. Very becoming are rolled or flared collars with curved edges that add thickness and width to thin necks.

15. The size of a collar must be scaled to the size of the wearer, and the shape must be flattering to the shape of the wearer's face and neck.

16. Yokes all the way across the front or back of the garment will widen the figure, and tend to emphasize the bustline or round shoulders.

17. A soft rolling collar, generous flat collar, bolero, cape, or short, straight jacket is flattering to the figure having round shoulders.

18. Bulky versions of pockets and bows will cover hollow chests.

19. Draped, bias necklines are not good for the figure with a large bust.

20. A figure with sloping or narrow shoulders may be built out with shoulder shapes. A wide, high lapel also helps to create the illusion of a straighter line. As we have learned, this figure is not good in dolman sleeves.

21. With a large bustline wear a bodice with slightly draped fullness or ease, rather than one which is revealingly smooth and tight. Such a bustline may also be broken by some vertical or diagonal movement.

22. A rounded, low collar is not good for a large, low bust. Choose a wide collar at the shoulder line.

23. Easy, bloused waistlines are good for the tall, thin figure.

24. Soft tucks or gathers are preferred at the waistline of the bodice for the figure that has a roll above the waistline or a large rib cage.

25. A straight-lined sheath will also accent the above disturbing line at the waistline.

26. Today's fashion calls for a normal shoulder line; therefore, if you do not have normal shoulders, use shoulder shapes (pp. 158–159, *The Bishop Method of Clothing Construction*). If only one shoulder is out of line, just one shoulder shape will be needed.

27. A curved line will add roundness and weight where it falls on the figure. If the line is directly over the bust, it gives an illusion of a full bust.

28. Points are slenderizing to the figure, for they lead the eye up and down in the direction of the point. The edge of a sleeve that is shaped into a point will slenderize a heavy arm. A long V at a neckline is flattering to a short neck and round face. Points which extend into the skirt decrease the width of the hips. A point extending from the shoulder in the direction of the waist increases the apparent width of the shoulder and minimizes the waist.

29. A beautiful bodice to a dress must have definition of fit and must also be in perfect line for the individual figure.

**The lines of your skirt.** 1. The length of your skirt has a great deal to do with the appearance of your legs. When skirts are short, they will be more flattering if they end as nearly as possible to the widest part of your back leg muscle; the legs will then taper gracefully from hemline to ankles. This point occurs at different heights on different people.

2. Don't lose chic by having a full skirt too long. A flared, pleated, or gathered skirt may be shorter than the straight skirt.

3. Straight or moderately wide skirts are much more slimming than wide ones.

4. Three or four gores in the front and in the back are better in proportion for a large figure that enlarges when seated, rather than one or two gores.

5. Two gores in the back are more becoming for the figure that can wear such a slim skirt than one piece in the back. The skirt will also hang and wear better. You may add a center seam when cutting the garment, if the pattern is cut all in one.

6. A wide skirt will make a small waist look even smaller.

7. If you are tall, you will look well in the widening look of unpressed pleats. If you are short, they are not for you unless they are modified.

8. Tubular, bouffant silhouettes in skirts when softened with pleats, peplums, tiers, or tunics give an effect of flowing grace for the tall, thin girl.

9. If your hips are too large, do emphasize your shoulders and neckline. Do not use hip decorations, such as patch pockets on both sides of the skirt. Skirts should be simple, easy, soft in line, and never tight or narrow.

10. For the smaller and more youthful figure with large hips, an equally pleasing effect may be produced by keeping the bodice and waist trim, and covering up the heaviness of the hip with a modified full skirt.

11. A prominent abdomen can be minimized with slight fullness in the skirt on either side of the protrusion, or with a finger-tip length jacket.

12. The bustle silhouette returns every so often. It is always a limited fashion, because few people are tall enough and thin enough to wear it well.

13. Bias-cut skirts are figure-revealing, and are difficult for the majority to wear smartly. They are also a problem to keep straight at the hemline in most fabrics.

14. More women look better with released tucks in the front of a skirt instead of stitched darts. Where they are placed depends on the individual figure.

15. The standard length of darts on patterns and ready-to-wear will frequently need to be adjusted for most individuals. To be most becoming, they should end short of the fullest part of the figure, such as the bust and hips.

16. The length of pleats must be in correct proportion to the height of the individual figure.

17. Pockets of bulky versions will cover bony hips.

18. Overblouses are widening to your hips, especially when in contrast.

19. Square corners on the lower edge of a jacket will be more slenderizing to your hips than rounded or slanted ones.

20. If you have wide hips, never narrow your shoulders. This makes your hips seem awkwardly large by comparison. If your hips are exceedingly wide, use sharp contrast only at the top of your figure—in your hat, at your neckline, across your shoulders—and wear dark colors with simple lines.

21. A short overskirt or a side drape decreases the apparent height of the wearer and adds width to the skirt.

22. The width of a waistband on a skirt is determined by the set of the figure at the waistline and by the height of the individual.

23. A beautiful skirt to a dress must have definition of fit and be in perfect line for the individual figure.

24. Nevertheless, in order to look well dressed, you must be comfortable in your clothes and look as if you are able to move inside them. Beauty today comes from simplicity and comfort in dress.

### The fabric you select

Fabric must be chosen to be right for the time of day and year, for the occasions for which it will be worn, for the figure, and for the pattern to be used. Color has been discussed in Chapter 1, "The Well-Dressed Woman."

1. Examples of daytime fabrics are flannel, wool crepe, tweed, silk linen, wool jersey, cotton, linen, and miracle fabrics.

2. Examples of fabrics for traditional occasions (big evenings and weddings) are satins, lace, organdy, brocade, velvet, and chiffon. Lace, chiffon, peau de soie, and taffeta can be worn the year around. Particularly appropriate for fall and winter are velvet, satin, and brocades; and for spring and summer, thin prints, organza, and organdy. Be careful about your fabric choices for evening. A solid color, perhaps crepe or faille, stands out in a group, and can be worn more often than something with much pattern and design. The lines should be simple and never cluttered.

3. Never use glittery, metallic fabrics for daytime wear.

4. Silk, linen, and wool are marvelous, rich fabrics: silk drapes well; linen is strong and durable; and wool is conforming and enduring.

5. Jersey is a wonderful fabric, but because of its characteristics, the pattern should be chosen carefully (see page 97, *The Bishop Method of Clothing Construction*). If the pattern is not chosen wisely, jersey will cling and be figure-revealing. Suit-weight wool jersey has much character. If you are planning a trip, add jersey to your selection. It will pack easily, travel well, go anywhere, and wear a long time.

6. Many cottons require too much pressing.

7. Thick, bulky, or shiny fabrics are not good on a large, heavy figure. Not only will shiny fabrics increase the apparent size of the figure, but they will reveal all the contours of the body and accentuate the lines in the face. Velvets and velveteens increase size because of their pile surface. Dull, broken-surfaced fabrics, such as heavy crepes, will absorb the light and reduce apparent size. Bulky, napped, and pile fabrics will add inches through their thickness and rounded folds. The large, heavy figure should never wear stiff, crisp, wiry, sheer, clinging, or flimsy fabrics, since they increase the size of the wearer. Good choices are lightweight tweeds, sheer woolens, heavy silk, wool crepes, semisheers, and linen.

8. A tall, thin girl needs napped fabric and soft fabrics that drape.

9. Transparent fabrics are figure-revealing unless used in several thicknesses. They are never attractive with buttons, buttonholes, and facings.

10. A hard finished, worsted fabric is not a good choice for an older person.

11. Harsh, firm, unyielding fabric is not good on the figure that is difficult to fit.

12. Stiff fabrics, such as taffeta or faille, will not yield for set-in sleeves; raglan or cut-on sleeves will continue in fashion for this reason alone. Stiff fabrics, unlike soft ones, do not lend themselves to any straight, closely fitted line.

13. Fine fabrics, such as silk, should never have a lot of cutting and stitching done on them with intricate designs in a pattern.

14. Surface fabric with an interesting texture should never be chopped up.

15. Some fabrics can be combined beautifully, such as a gray flannel suit with a white satin vest or blouse, a wool crepe suit with a silk print lining and blouse, or a printed silk dress with a wool crepe jacket. A coat of a tweed fabric should never be worn over a satin dress.

16. Many fabrics handle well in soft, heavy folds. Often a fabric such as voile would have little texture interest when used on flat surfaces, but it gains distinction when its surfaces are broken into tucks and folds. Chiffon and georgette hang in a similar way to voile.

17. Heavier satins, taffetas, and failles take on a look of elegance.

18. Wool, silk, and velvets lend themselves to small folds in a soft, clinging fashion.

19. Remember always the importance of selecting fabric carefully. It must have the right weight or body for good results in the job to be done.

20. Analyze fabric by the yard or in a dress by holding it up to your face before buying it.

21. A black or navy dinner dress in a lightweight wool or in silk crepe is a must in everyone's wardrobe.

## If you choose a design

We are discussing here the choice of prints, polka dots, stripes, and plaids for the individual. Once chosen, what consideration should be given to the way they are made up, and where should they be worn?

1. When making up a garment from design, the structural lines must be kept simple. Emphasize the importance of the design. You liked the fabric when you bought it; so the design should be kept in first place, and the lines kept simple. Many structural lines of a dress are lost in the design.

2. Study the design of your fabric and see if it will tell you what to do. The design of the dress should harmonize with the design of the fabric, and it may even suggest its own trim.

3. Reversible prints, brown on white in a dress, white on brown in a jacket, are popular in today's fashion.

4. Two opposing designs should never be worn together, such as a plaid skirt with a print blouse.

5. You will tire quickly of bold prints and plaids or large checks and stripes. Ascertain if it will be possible to match the design of the plaid in the lines of the pattern you select (see pages 96–97, *The Bishop Method of Clothing Construction*).

6. If you are tall and thin, you can wear a large blanket plaid, but if you are short and stout, avoid it.

7. Bold stripes and polka dots are considered *hard* in appearance for many people to wear. Perhaps, using them for a trim on a garment (overcollar and cuffs on a suit) would be a smarter choice than using them for the entire garment. Yet, while coin dots may seem to be too much, polka dots, scattered or small, are easy to wear. Polka dots unevenly spaced are usually more interesting in design.

8. Choose vertical stripes if you feel that horizontal stripes make you look wide.

9. On a heavy figure, prints should be small in design against a darker background. Polka dots should be very small. Prints that lead the eye in a circular or swirling movement suggest rotundity. Prints that are widely spaced and in strong contrast attract attention to size.

10. With a two-color tweed or check (such as black and white), the garment generally becomes more interesting when both colors are brought out separately in the costume as sharp contrasts. An example is a white collar with a black binding. However, the sharp contrasts may be done with accessories.

11. With a bright design, any contrast would be a dark color in the fabric to tone it down, such as a black velvet bow or belt. With a subdued design, any contrast would be a bright color to pick it up, such as yellow linen lapels on a jacket.

12. Avoid straight seams in a check or stripe when selecting your pattern. With red and white check, for example, a straight seam may bring together two red or two white lines; this will not be pleasing.

13. We must learn to recognize good prints, to select them to be right for the occasion, and to have them express the personality of the wearer. Many women are afraid to wear prints; they feel that prints compete with their faces, figures, and personality. They are surely right unless they know how to select the proper ones.

14. Women very often look cooler in solid colors than in prints.

15. A few well-dressed women rarely wear prints, while others have them in their wardrobe the year around. Whatever is your choice, the following facts must be recognized.

a. Strictly realistic treatment of animal and plant forms and of scenic landscapes are never suitable for wearing apparel. Good prints may have their motifs based on nature, but the designer will have added something creative of his own. In other words, choose an artist's print rather than a gardener's.

b. The shapes or motifs should be interesting in contour, and so arranged as to make a pleasing rhythm.

c. The spaces which form the background areas must have interest in themselves so that the fabric as a whole will be pleasing.

d. Do not purchase a print that lacks any particular significance.

e. Prints suggest different things to us. Some are so exotic, bright, and unusual as to be suitable only for gala social evenings, vacations, or cruise wear. Others give the impression they belong to youth and are gay and amusing. Many seem dainty, refined, ladylike, as though they were intended for delicate, feminine women. Certain allover prints give the impression of force, vigor, and drama, suggesting their use by sophisticated, dignified women. Finally, there are those that are conventional and conservative, admirably suggesting the conservatism needed by the mature woman or one in business.

# Chapter 3

# Alterations of ready-to-wear

We have had countless requests to do this chapter in our second book, because surprisingly few people know how clothes should fit. In putting together this chapter, we have tried to show the most common alterations necessary for the majority of people.

Whether you do the alterations yourself or have someone do them for you, it is important to know how clothes should fit! The average individual wants things much too tight, while others want them too loose. A garment that is too tight will accent every figure fault and will make your figure appear larger. You should always conceal rather than reveal your figure defects. Furthermore, there must never be any strain on the crosswise or lengthwise, or the garment will never look or feel comfortable.

Even the most expensive clothes can never have a quality look, unless they fit well. Alterations are not difficult, if you just know how they should be done.

Clothes are manufactured in many different types and sizes—Junior, Misses', Women's, Half-size, Diminuettes, Petites, etc. Learn what is best for your figure. A common alteration is to change a regular size into a half-size, but you should avoid it, if you can.

In addition, you should remember that the style of the garment governs what alterations can be made. In other words, you must consider whether the alterations will impair the style of the garment. Or, stated in another way, you must understand the silhouette of the garment to judge the alterations wisely.

Then, too, the lines and details must be right for the proportion of the individual figure. Many people buy clothes because they like them, and give no thought to whether they can or cannot be fitted to their figure.

Clothes that fit properly are comfortable. You can forget yourself in them, be self-assured, and at your best. Compared to the past, comfort and freedom are highlights of today's fashion.

The right style of foundation garments and a proper fit for the individual figure are extremely important in helping you to determine what alterations will be necessary.

When you have made a decision to purchase a garment in a store, the fitter is called. Then, just as the fitter has the prerogative to turn down a sale if she thinks the garment cannot be altered properly, so do you, if you feel the fitting will be too involved after the suggestions are made. To make a garment look fashion right is a fitter's business, but it is also your personal concern. Too many alterations are always questionable.

However, more women are learning to do their alterations at home, because the cost of alterations continues to increase. For example, in one large department store, out of 49 garment sales, 10 are pin-fittings to be done elsewhere. This same store had 55 fitters ten years ago, 30 four years ago, and 17 today. The majority of the stores report between 40% and 50% of their transactions are pin-fittings. Yet, some of the alterations have been minimized in recent years because of the many types of clothes on the market. The consensus of opinion among alteration departments is that faulty manufacturing very materially affects alteration costs. Sometimes, garments are even sent back to manufacturers because the cut is wrong. If the garment is cut off grain, it can never fit anyone nor ever be right in line. Thus the wise shopper will always be grain conscious.

The most common and routine alterations are at the waistline, side seams, and hems. Next in line are adjusting shoulders and correcting sleeve lengths. A garment that fits the upper part of the body is the best buy; skirt alterations are easy. Shoulder and neckline alterations are more difficult and are apt to be less satisfactory than skirt alterations. They are also more expensive than skirt alterations.

In altering skirts, fitters often find that one hip is very unlike the other. It is usually easier and safer to take in a garment than to let it out. Seams that must be let out may present problems. The matching notches may be cut into them, the seams may be too narrow, they may show stitch marks, and they may have shine on the wrong side that cannot be removed.

Bust darts are lowered instead of raised 95% of the time in altering ready-to-wear. Sloped ones are better than straight ones on the majority.

Hem alterations usually cost from $2.00 to $7.00; adjusting sleeve lengths, from $2.00 to $4.00. Naturally, alteration prices vary with the section of the country. A machine hem in an alteration department costs less than a hand hem. It costs extra when there is an underlining in a dress. There is a machine that cuts the hem the correct width, and sews on the tape at the same time. Always be aware that hems cannot be let down if the underneath corners are cut away. Then, too, a full skirt will always appear to be longer than a slim one of exactly the same length, since the latter tends to ride up as you walk. It is interesting to note that one large department store altered 22,787 garments in 1960. Of these, 85.6% had hem alterations, but may have had other alterations, also. One-third of these hems were done by hand, and two-thirds by machine. That represented 25% of their business transactions.

We did not include anything on finishing hems in this chapter, because once a ready-made garment would be marked for shortening or lengthening, you would choose the hem finish most desirable for the fabric, as presented on pages 46, 82, and 142–143, *The Bishop Method of Clothing Construction.*[*]

Almost no one is a perfect size. The chances that any ready-made garment will fit many women perfectly are very slim indeed.

All the suggestions offered in Chapter 7, *BMCC*, on "Fitting and Cutting-to-Fit" should help in understanding this chapter. However, all of them cannot be used in altering ready-to-wear, because you are very limited in what can be done after the garment is cut out.

We would like to call your particular attention to two sections on pages 47–48, *BMCC*, describing what is meant by a perfect-fitting garment, and then how a garment is handled when tried on for a fitting.

[*]Through the remainder of this chapter, this text will be referred to as *BMCC*.

**1.** The shoulder seam should lie on top of the figure—as if to cut the figure in half. That placement will be one inch behind the lobe of the ear.

Since the shoulder seam comes too far to the front on this dress, the back seam can be taken in, and the front seam let out as much as possible. For perfect alignment, the dress in the photograph looks as if it will need ¾ inch let out on the front, but the seam allowance may not give that much.

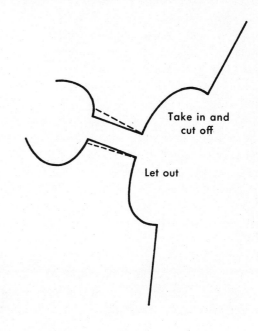

Take in and cut off

Let out

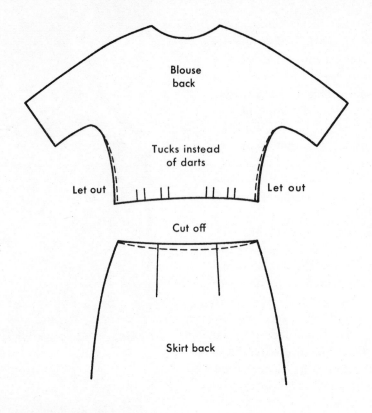

Blouse back

Tucks instead of darts

Let out         Let out

Cut off

Skirt back

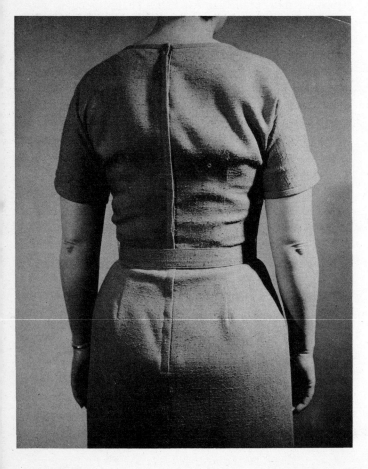

**2.** This figure needs more width in the back of the bodice. The seam allowance can be let out gradually at the sides of the back, and the darts changed to tucks to give additional ease. The softer bloused effect with tucks will be more becoming for this figure.

To eliminate the wrinkle at the center back of the skirt below the belt, the skirt can be cut out at the center back.

In making a dress for this figure, the skirt would need more width and height at the side back as indicated with sketch 6, page 67, and sketch 10, page 69, *BMCC*.

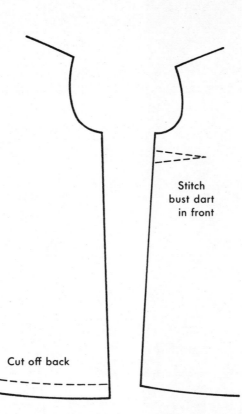

Stitch
bust dart
in front

Cut off back

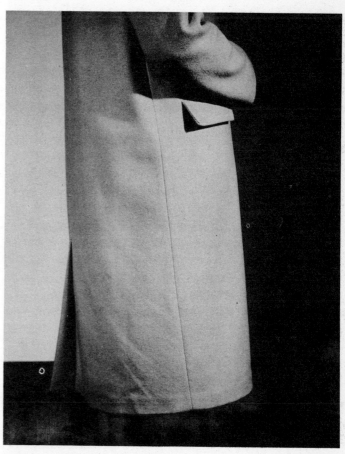

**3.** When the side seam swings toward the front on a coat and the hemline drops at the back, the problem will be corrected by adding a bust dart. It should be made in line with the crown of the bust, and the same amount taken up in the dart must be cut off the coat back before the side seams are re-stitched. This coat looks as if it swings toward the front about two inches.

The pleat would be better if it lapped right over left because it would always have less strain when sliding under the wheel of a car, etc.

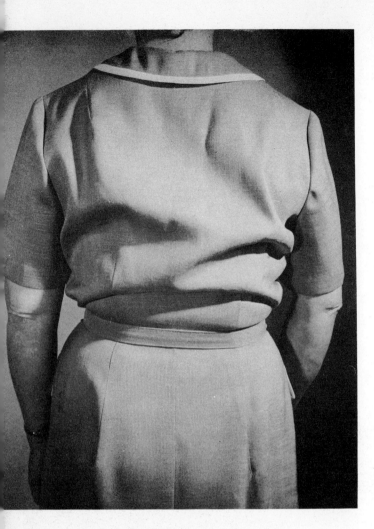

**4.** There may even be too much to alter in the back of this bodice, but what it needs is excess fabric cut off all the way across the bottom. A bust dart can be made in the front of the bodice, and if necessary, a small amount can be trimmed off the bottom of the front so that the side seams of the bodice will match with perfection.

This arm would look smarter if the sleeve were one or one and one-half inches longer.

The darts are too deep in the back of the skirt for this figure. They should be decreased and shortened, and the difference cut off the side seams of the skirt back. This is a common alteration.

Decrease and
shorten darts and
cut off side seam
of back only

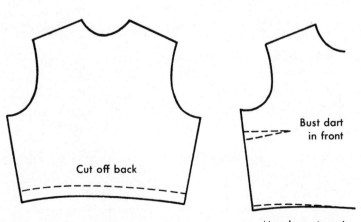

Cut off back

Bust dart
in front

May have to cut
off some here

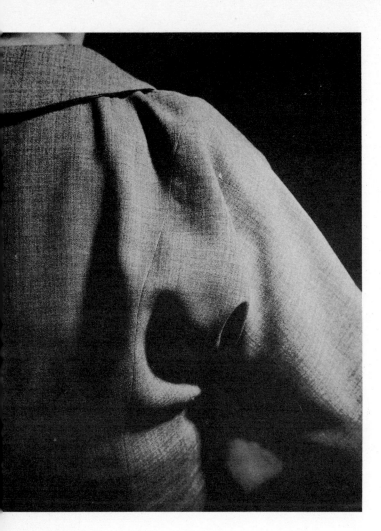

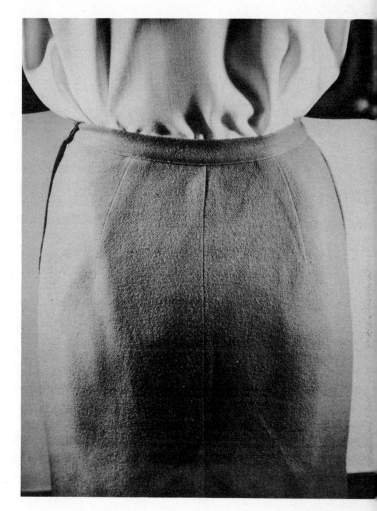

**6.** The curved hip darts accentuate the hip line, so this figure would be improved greatly if the darts were made straighter and two shorter ones were used instead of the one long and deep dart.

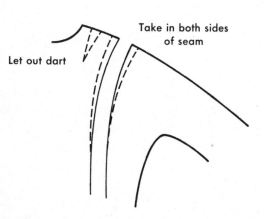

Let out dart

Take in both sides of seam

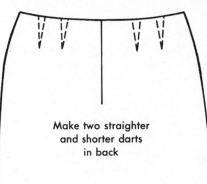

Make two straighter and shorter darts in back

**5.** The back shoulder dart that is showing below the collar should be taken out, because it is pulling the back off grain. Then, both sides of the seam should be taken in. We have many cut-on sleeves in the fashion picture, but they can present as many fitting problems as set-in sleeves.

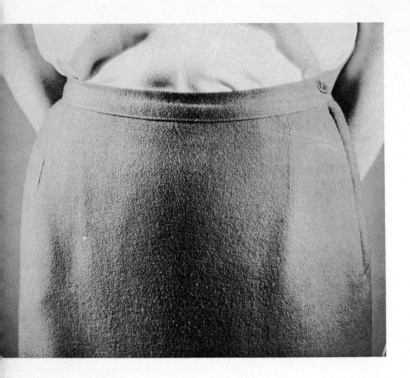

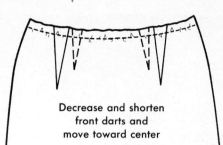

Decrease and shorten
front darts and
move toward center

**7.** The darts on the front of this skirt are too far apart and give the figure a wide look. The skirt was also too straight when it was sewn on the band.

To correct these, decrease the darts and move them closer to the center. Ease the difference at the waistline when stitching the skirt to the band.

Tucks or folds could be used on the front of this skirt instead of the darts.

**8.** This is a rather typical look in ready-to-wear. The pocket pulls apart because the skirt is too tight in the hips. It will not help to decrease the darts in the skirt front. Normally, the seams of the pocket and skirt are trimmed away, so it would not be possible to let the skirt out at the pocket edges. It is not wise to purchase shorts, slacks, dresses, or skirts that are tight in the hips and have pockets in the seams, because nothing can be done to correct the problem.

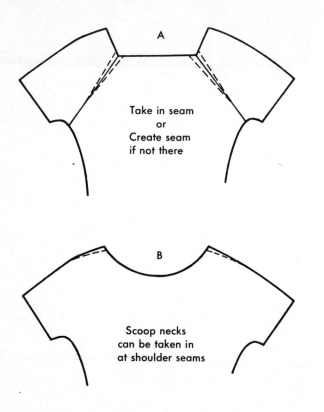

A

Take in seam
or
Create seam
if not there

B

Scoop necks
can be taken in
at shoulder seams

**9.** If a low neckline is loose or wide in the front, several things can be done to help correct it, depending upon the amount of the problem and style of the dress. In sketch A, the seams of the dress could be taken in deeper. In altering ready-to-wear, this seam is sometimes created in front or back or both places if it isn't already there in the style of the dress.

Sketch B indicates that larger necklines can also be taken in at the shoulder seams. This may have to be done equally all the way out on the seam. Sometimes the facing is taken off, and the neckline is eased. Then, the facing is made smaller before it is put back on the dress.

**10.** The bodice darts (A) from the waistline are too high; at no time should they come up over the crown of the bust. When the figure is low busted, it is better to change the bodice darts into two tucks.

This figure does not have enough bust for the depth of the bust darts (B); so they should be decreased, and the bodice shortened all the way across the front. Decreasing the dart will also help the side seam of the front fit the side seam of the back.

The skirt front is tight looking and needs tucks or folds instead of darts. Lifting the skirt front (a result of shortening the bodice, as the diagram shows) will straighten the tabs.

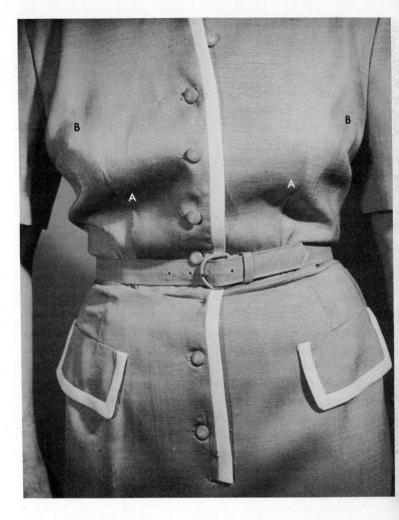

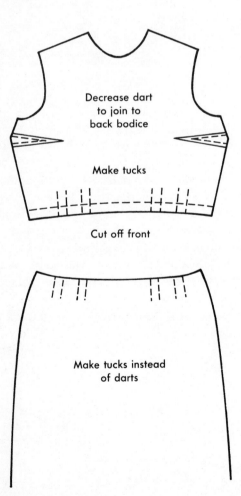

Decrease dart
to join to
back bodice

Make tucks

Cut off front

Make tucks instead
of darts

**11.** The sleeve is wrinkling because it needs to come forward in the armhole. The pin at A shows the amount the sleeve should be moved to the shoulder seam at B to straighten the grain across the sleeve cap.

The front shoulder is too wide and is falling off the shoulder bone. However, there is no extra width on the back, as the next photograph clearly indicates. Trim off the excess fabric as the sketch illustrates. The back shoulder seam will be eased to the front. When the side seam of the back of the jacket is cut down, as the next sketch indicates, it will be necessary to lessen the front darts.

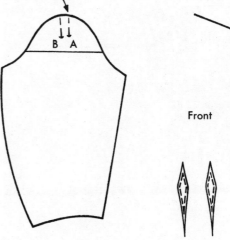

**12.** This figure is short-waisted. The pins at A identify the deepest part of the curved seams for the waistline, but for this figure the waistline curve needs to be reshaped so that the deepest part will be at B. (See sketch.) This will eliminate the long look of the back.

It would be an expensive alteration to fit the rest of the jacket back, because the collar and sleeves would have to be removed to cut away the excess fabric, as the sketch illustrates.

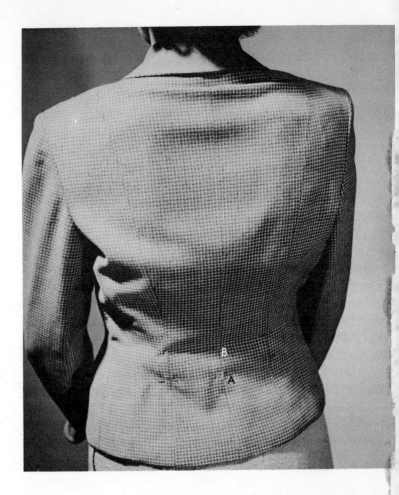

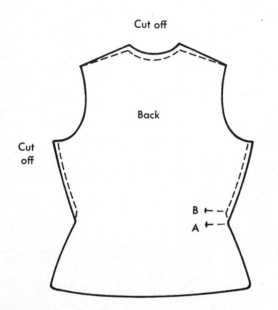

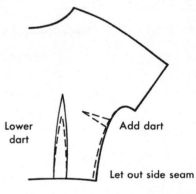

**13.** The sleeve length is attractive on this arm. The main fitting problem with the dress is that it is too tight in the bust. First, the bodice dart (A) should be lowered to end below the crown of the bust. It is robbing the figure of fabric that is there. Then, a bust dart must be added. The side seams of the bodice will still meet, because the back bodice will be shortened, as the next sketch points out.

Considering how tight this bodice is in the bust by the way it pulls at the buttons and buttonholes, it would not even be advisable to buy it unless there was enough seam to let out under the arm.

**14.** The way this dress wrinkles high and low in the back is typical of much of the look with ready-to-wear. To give more width across the back, the darts should be changed to two tucks. The extra length in the bodice would be cut off the bottom. The side seams of the bodice will still meet, because the front bodice needs a bust dart added, as the former sketch illustrated.

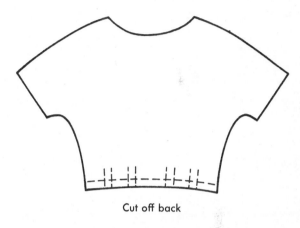

Cut off back

**15.** If a dress fits properly in the front of a bodice, but the back bodice is this much too long, do not buy it, because it could not be altered satisfactorily. In the preceding photograph and sketch, the alteration was feasible because the front of the dress needed a bust dart.

When shopping for ready-to-wear, it can be discouraging if the figure needs two sizes larger for the hips than the bodice. Sometimes, the side seams of the skirt can be let out enough, as the first sketch on the next page illustrates.

Do not buy a dress two sizes larger to fit the hips if the bodice must be made that much smaller. Such an alteration would be expensive and is not even recommended.

**16.** The front of this skirt is too tight in the hips, just as the former photograph illustrated with the back. The side seams can be let out, if there is sufficient allowance, and the extra width at the waistline put into more gathers, or extra tucks or darts if the dress had them instead of gathers.

The bustline is too low on this figure for the curve of this dress, so the curve needs to be relocated.

At A, the front of the sleeve needs to be dropped and cut off to straighten the line of the sleeve. Then, the sleeve would be hemmed again.

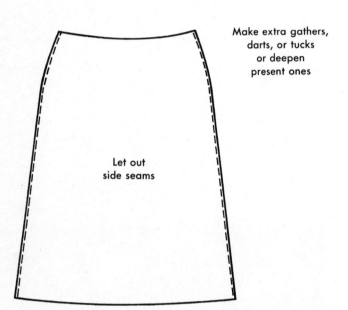

Make extra gathers, darts, or tucks or deepen present ones

Let out side seams

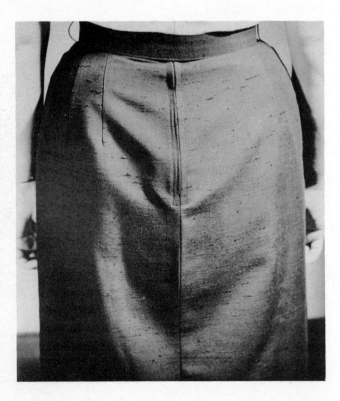

Straight of grain

Shorten and curve darts

**17.** The way this skirt cups at the back is a typical American look. To straighten the grain at the hipline, as the sketch illustrates, the skirt needs to be lifted at the center back. The right hip is even higher than the left hip. Then, the darts should be shortened and curved in stitching.

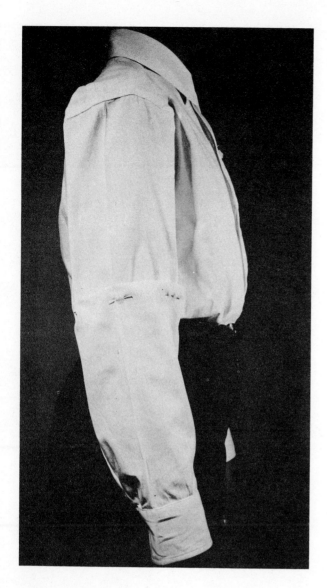

**18.** The correct sleeve length for a shirt is judged when the arm is down; there should not be a break in either the cuff or the sleeve. The tuck that is pinned in this shirt is to show how much the sleeve needs to be shortened.

Never take off the cuff to shorten the sleeve; always take out the sleeve at the armhole and cut off excess length at the top of the sleeve.

On less expensive shirts, it may be necessary to take in the underarm seam of the shirt (see sketch) so that the smaller cap will fit the armhole, or to add little pieces to the sleeve underarm. However, more expensive shirts have ease on the sleeve cap, and neither of these may be necessary, depending upon the amount the sleeve is shortened.

**19.** The back of this dress is entirely too short waisted. If there is sufficient seam allowance in the blouse, let it down as much as possible. The only other alternative is to wear a wide belt to cover the short-waisted look.

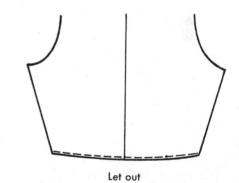

Let out

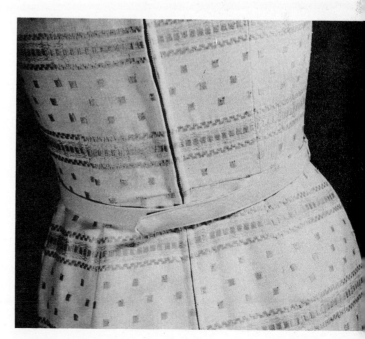

May have to take in here

Cut off

**20.** Two alterations are necessary on the front of this skirt. First, the front needs to be lifted and cut out at the center, tapering to nothing at the side seams. Then, the skirt will be more becoming on the figure if the fullness is arranged in two tucks or folds instead of gathers, and if they are placed closer to the front of the skirt.

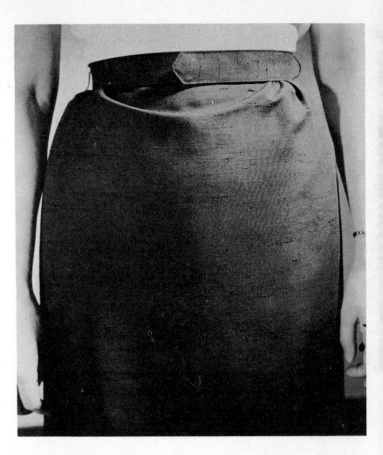

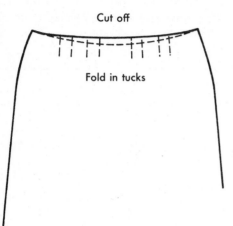

Cut off

Fold in tucks

**21.** This figure definitely has a high right hip. If this skirt were being made, the pin on the waistband shows how much would be added to the skirt at the right top in cutting, tapering to nothing at the center back. However, in altering ready-to-wear, the only thing that can be done to straighten the skirt is to lift the left side as the sketch illustrates. The bottom of a pleated skirt must always be hemmed on grain, just as we say of a gathered skirt on page 112, *BMCC*.

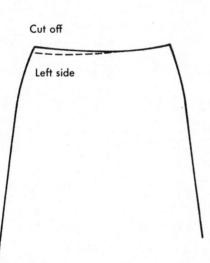

Cut off

Left side

**22.** The Ivy League style of this dress is very popular, and this tight look at the waistline is common with it. Some of the fabric in the tucks should be let out, and some ease should be allowed on the bodice when it is restitched to the skirt. The wrinkles underarm will disappear when the bodice is loosened below. The remaining fabric from the tucks should be made into two smaller tucks on each side, and they should be closer to the side seams. If a figure has prominent shoulders, a bloused line at the waistline is always more becoming.

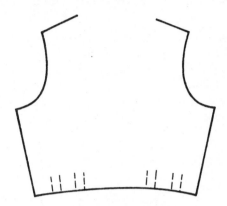

Make smaller tucks
toward side edges
Ease to skirt

**23.** This photograph illustrates another typical ready-to-wear look in the fit of the bodice. The bust dart (A) needs to be relocated so that it is in line with the crown of the bust. Then, the bodice darts (B) must be lowered so that they end under the crown of the bust. The midriff is too tight; so the bodice darts should be decreased at the same time they are being lowered, and the side seams of the front bodice let out. Then, the bodice can be eased to the skirt when the waistline seam is restitched.

There is enough width in the skirt below the darts, but the darts should be decreased so that the skirt would be eased when restitched to the tape at the waistline. This will eliminate the tight look in the skirt front below the belt.

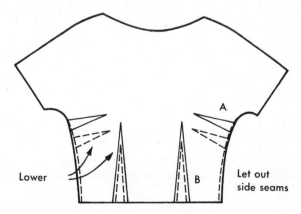

Lower                    Let out
side seams

33

**24.** Trousers in the correct length do not have any break at the top of the cuffs. To alter the length of them, remove stitching and crease marks in present cuffs. Turn the bottom to the right side (A) at the correct length. Pin evenly all around and then press this line.

Measure up 1½ inches from this line and fold down (B). This line is the edge of the cuff, and should be pressed, also. Turn under the remaining length to the inside (C) and stitch to the underside of trousers. Press again (D) and the cuff is finished.

Turn down the cuff at the sides (E) and hand-stitch the cuff to the trousers about ½ inch from the top of the cuff.

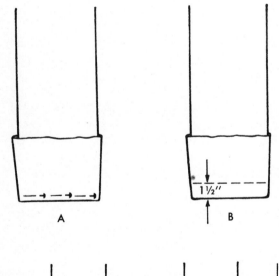

A      B

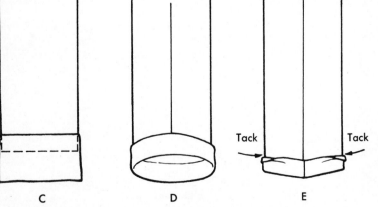

C      D      E

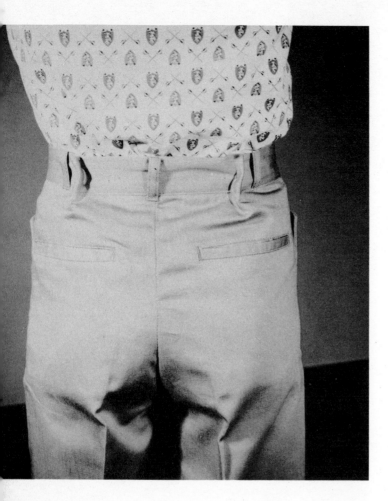

**25.** When trousers are too large at the waistline, they may be altered in two ways. First, there are normally darts in the design, which can be deepened where the tucks are pinned. If not, darts can be stitched on the inside to take out the excess at the area where the tucks are pinned. This is done on children's trousers so that the darts can be let out easily as the child develops.

The other method, and the one usually followed for an adult, is to make the alteration at the center back seam, unless it is so much that it pulls the trousers out of line.

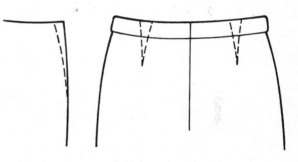

**26.** Any style of jacket should always hang with perfect straight of grain at the two front edges, as the sketch indicates. This jacket is being pulled out of line because the hips are large. The darts should be decreased—maybe even let out altogether to the waistline and just be stitched above. Then, if necessary, the side seams may also be let out.

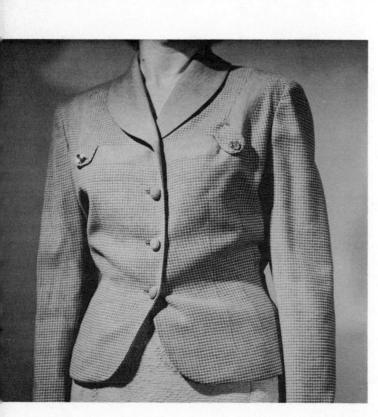

Let out darts maybe altogether up to waist

Let out side seam

**27.** Even if there were sufficient fabric in the seam of this sleeve to let it out enough for a comfortable size in the upper arm, it would be an expensive alteration in a lined garment.

To shorten the sleeve the amount indicated by the pinned tuck, the cuff would have to be removed. This would also be an expensive alteration.

Neither of these is recommended.

**28.** The darts are entirely too high and too long for this figure, and they are too deep. Notice the fullness at both ends of the darts. When they are decreased in stitching, the back side seams can then be made deeper to take in the excess fabric. The line of this dress would have been improved with a center back seam.

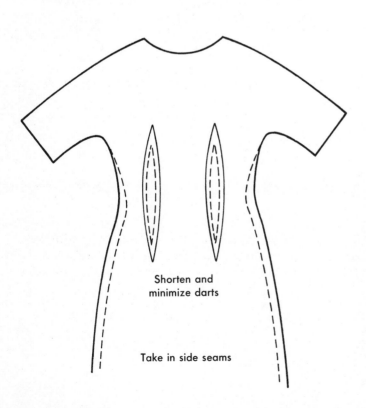

Shorten and
minimize darts

Take in side seams

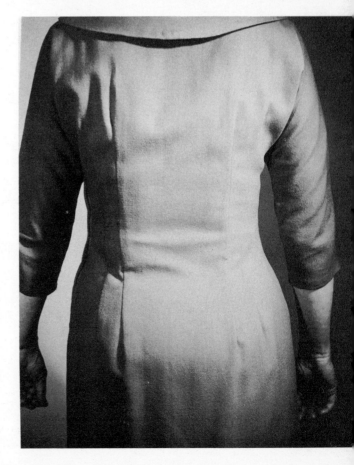

**29.** The way this shoulder pulls up at the front is a common shoulder problem. The front shoulder seam needs to be let out, but it would not be a recommended alteration for this dress because the collar line would never be right at the front. Always study the line of your garment to analyze if it can be altered. Never buy a garment that has straight of grain (A in sketch) at the shoulder line of a cut-on sleeve, as this dress does. It will never hang right when your arms are down. The shoulder line of the sleeve should always be cut with a bias line (B in sketch).

When ready-made clothes do not fit, it is due to our figure differences from the model figure, or to the poor cut of the garment. This dress has examples of both of these.

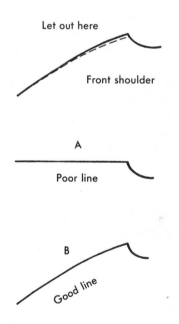

**30.** The detail in the design of this dress, with the fan-shaped darts at the bustline, would make it impossible to alter this dress through the bustline and have a quality look. It is not recommended.

# Chapter 4

# Complete or back drums in skirts or dresses

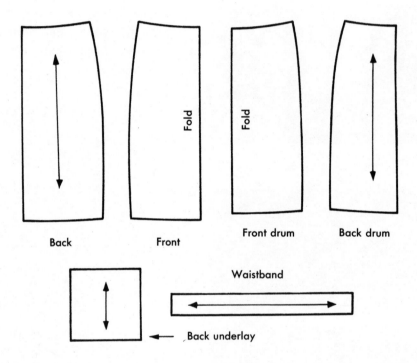

Back    Front    Front drum    Back drum

Waistband

Back underlay

A seam opening in the back of a skirt with an underlay on the skirt drum has replaced pleats for walking room. The seam opening is smarter looking and is easier to maintain. It also reduces bulk in many fabrics, and it does not pull out of shape as pleats sometimes do.

With a fabric like wool, always use a complete drum. With fabric like cotton, just the back drum is preferred because of ease in laundering.

The complete or back drum is recommended in straight skirts, not only for the underlay at the seam opening, but for several other reasons. It helps skirts to retain their shape, gives more character to the appearance of the finished garment, and many times

eliminates wearing a half-slip. A blouse or camisole is all that is needed with a suit skirt that has a complete drum.

Complete drums are made from firm rayon fabrics; a twill is a good choice. Suracel is highly recommended. Back drums are made from super soft or soft siri, or from one of the many synthetic, cotton, or silk underlinings on the market.

Drums are cut from the same pattern pieces as the skirt and on the identical grain. It is worthy of mention that a selvage could never be used at the lower edge of a drum, as you may sometimes find in ready-to-wear, because the grain would be entirely incorrect.

## The complete drum

**Skirt front unit.** Staystitch waistline edge and sides of skirt from notch up just outside the seamline and in the direction arrows indicate.

**Skirt back unit.** Staystitch waistline edge and right side of skirt from notch up just outside seamline and in the direction arrows indicate. Staystitch left side of skirt from notch up ¼ inch from edge.

Front outside

Back outside

Back outside

With right sides together, baste-stitch along center back line from lower edge for the desired length of seam opening. Place a square of seam binding over end of seam opening, and changing to regulation stitch, lockstitch at end of opening through seam binding. Continue stitching along center back line to waistline. If A edges are not selvage, staystitch ⅜ inch from edges and pink with pinking shears. Stitch darts and press toward center back.

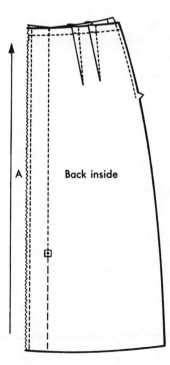

A    Back inside

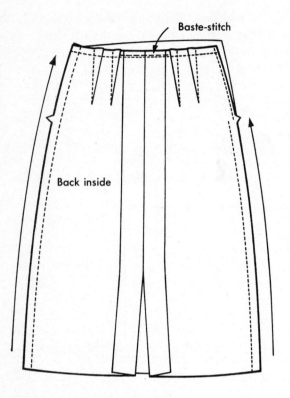

Baste-stitch

Back inside

**Complete skirt unit.** Press back edges open and baste-stitch to waist edge outside seamline. Remove baste-stitching below lockstitching at lower edge. Stitch side seams from lower edge to waist edge, leaving left side open exact length of metal part of zipper with tab turned up, plus waist seam allowance. Finish seams, if necessary, and press open.

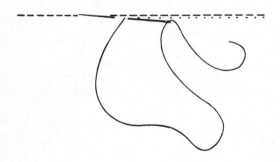

Insert zipper with the same learnings as on pp. 40–41, *The Bishop Method of Clothing Construction.*° Use hand-picking on front edge of placket instead of machine stitching.

You may baste-stitch last row of stitching on front edge as a guide for hand-picking. Then, baste-stitching can be removed when hand-picking is completed.

Do hand-picking from topside of skirt. Use buttonhole twist thread or double mercerized thread in needle. Draw thread through a beeswax holder. Bring needle to topside of fabric. Take stitch backward when putting needle to underside of fabric. Bring needle to topside of fabric about ¼ inch from first stitching. Continue hand-picking placket opening for a fine custom look. Remove baste-stitching.

°Throughout the remainder of this chapter this text will be referred to as *BMCC*.

This photograph shows the completed placket with hand-picking after the baste-stitching has been removed.

Open out back extension edges and using hem gauge, turn up hem and press. Finish hem like photograph on page 171, *BMCC*. If the edges of the seam opening were not cut on the selvage, apply a piece of seam tape turning under lower ends. Slipstitch inner edge to hem.

If you are making a dress, the drum will have to be staystitched to the skirt at the waistline (see steps to follow), and the bodice joined to the skirt, before the zipper can be inserted. For approximately 1½ inches from the zipper opening, snip drum to seamline at waistline, and keep free from waistline seam until zipper is inserted. Then, the drum may be hemmed by hand around the placket (page 103, *BMCC*), or finished the same as the technique that follows here.

**Front drum unit.** The drum is cut one inch shorter than the skirt. Staystitch waistline edge and sides of drum from notch up, just outside the seamline and in the direction arrows indicate.

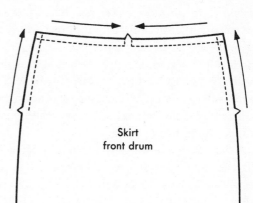

Skirt
front drum

## Complete or back drums

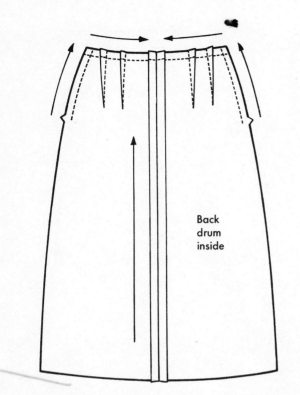

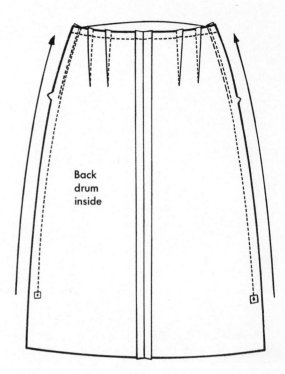

**Complete drum unit.** Staystitch waistline edge and sides of drum from notch up, just outside the seamline and in the direction arrows indicate.

With right sides together, stitch center back seam in direction shown. Finish with pinking shears, if necessary (this is cut on the selvage, when possible), and press open. Stitch darts and press toward side edges, opposite of the skirt darts.

Stitch side seams in direction shown, leaving them open at lower edge for three inches plus hem allowance for walking room. Place a square of seam binding at beginning of stitching, and lockstitch through it for added strength at opening.

Baste-stitch opening on right side for zipper placket; it will come on the left side when lining is put in skirt.

Finish seams with pinking shears, and press open. Stitch a strip of seam tape to raw edges of zipper opening; turn under raw ends at lower edge. Hem by hand to drum. Remove baste-stitching at placket opening.

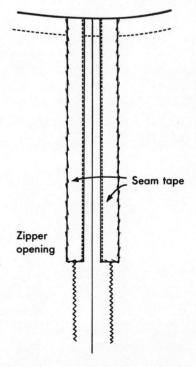

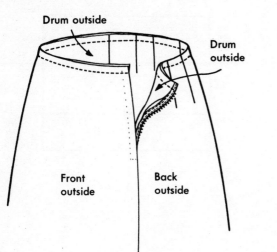

Drum outside

Drum outside

Front outside

Back outside

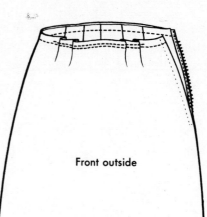

Front outside

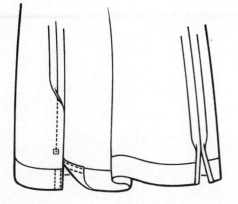

**Complete skirt unit.** With wrong sides together, pin drum to waist edge of skirt, keying centers and right side seam and placing side opening edges of drum over zipper on left side of skirt. Stitch waist edges together just outside seamline.

In the photograph on page 103, *BMCC*, the right side of the drum was placed to the wrong side of the skirt only because the dress was made from sheer wool and the drum was made from a firm taffeta.

Fold tucks on outside of skirt front through skirt and drum. Stitch tucks in place across waist edge.

Make the waistband and put it on the skirt exactly as you learned to do on page 170, *BMCC*.

Using hem gauge, turn up hem of drum and press. Finish like bottom photograph, page 46, *BMCC*. At side openings, stitch hem and drum together ⅝ inch from raw edge; staystitch raw edges ⅛ inch from edge. Press back seam allowance on ⅝-inch stitching line, turn under raw edges on ⅛-inch stitching line, and hem at machine, or slipstitch by hand. Drum will finish one inch shorter than skirt.

## Complete or back drums

**Skirt back underlay unit.**    Turn hem allowance on skirt back underlay to outside and stitch sides with ¼-inch seam for one inch from fold up.

Clip to end of stitching.

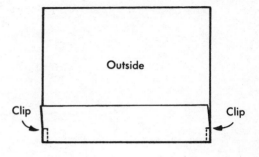

Turn hem to inside and press.   Pink remaining edges.   Finish hem same as skirt hem.

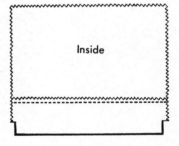

With wrong sides together, place underlay on back drum.   Topstitch ¼ inch from edge.   Underlay drops one inch below drum to finish same length as skirt.

When a complete drum is used in a lighter weight fabric, the underlay may be used all the way across the back drum, as it is when just a back drum is used (see page 47).

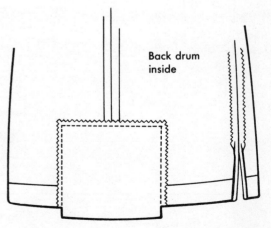

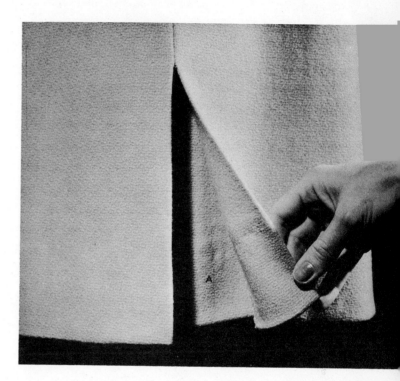

Final-press skirt (Chapter 9, *BMCC*).

This photograph shows the completed seam opening on outside of skirt. Underlay (A) is stitched to drum.

This photograph shows the completed drum and underlay. The skirt was turned wrong side out to take the photograph. When it is right side out, the underlay faces the wool skirt.

## Back skirt drum.

The skirt back unit is prepared exactly like the directions on page 39, except that back darts are stitched later. Before sewing side seams, however, staystitch the back drum to the back of the skirt.

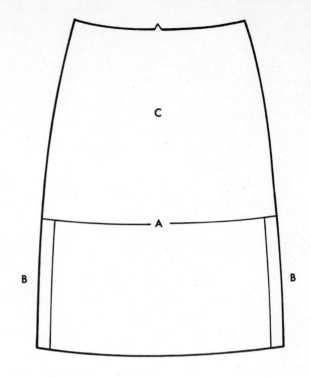

For approximately two inches above the seam opening at the back of the skirt, cut underlay of skirt fabric from same pattern as skirt back, and on identical grain. Omit the extension at center back and cut underlay on fold. Add ⅝-inch seam allowance to edge A, and cut off 1¼ inches from B edges. The underlay will finish the same length as the skirt. Cut drum area (C) from fabrics suggested at the beginning of this chapter. Cut like skirt back and on identical grain; add ⅝-inch seam allowance at A edge.

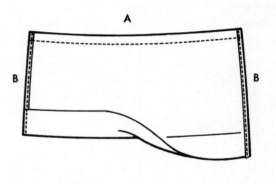

At B edges, staystitch ⅛ inch from edge. Turn in raw edges on staystitching and hem B edges at machine. One of the B edges may be cut on the selvage and will not require finishing. Turn up hem and finish same as skirt hem.

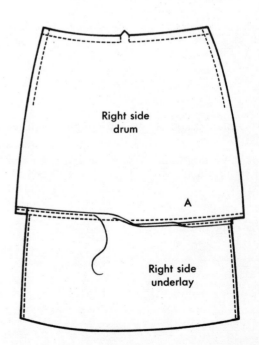

Staystitch A edges on underlay and drum just outside seamline. With wrong sides together, stitch ⅝-inch seam at A edge. Trim drum seam to scant ¼ inch. Staystitch seam allowance of underlay ¼ inch from raw edge, turn under seam allowance on staystitching, and stitch to drum in flat-felled seam.

Place right side of drum to inside of skirt back. Place flat and check that it will fit and conform in the back of the skirt with perfection. Pin in place. Then, the darts can be stitched in the back of the skirt. Staystitch to skirt at D and E edges outside seamline, and in direction arrows indicate. Staystitch ¼ inch from edge on left side from notch up for zipper opening. The darts in the drum are just laid into place at the waistline as tucks, and are not stitched down.

If a skirt style has 3 gores in the back, then both seams could have a seam opening as we have shown at the center back.

Proceed with stitching side seams and remainder of skirt construction.

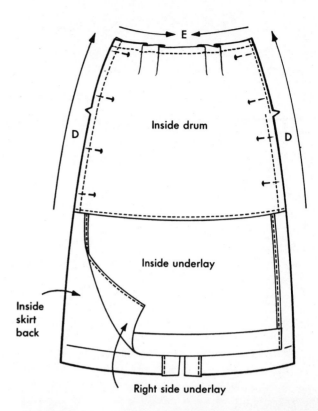

This photograph shows the completed drum in the back of the skirt.

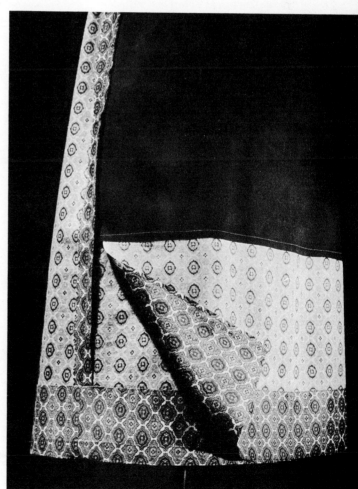

# Chapter 5

# Lined toppettes for women and girls

Toppettes (or overblouses, as they are sometimes called) are popular, attractive, and comfortable, not only for children, but for women as well. They are worn over bathing suits, for a distinct change on a straight-lined or sheath dress, and with short shorts, bermuda shorts, pedal pushers, and slacks.

We have shown both styles (sleeveless and with cut-on sleeves) double and reversible. It is fun to make them reversible when the fabrics contrast on the two sides.

The double construction helps the overblouses to retain their shape, gives more support for adding various trims, and is more pleasing in appearance in lightweight fabrics. It helps us to attain our ever important objective—the quality look!

You may be able to cut several overblouses from just little pieces of fabric you have at home, and you can have fun making them in one evening!

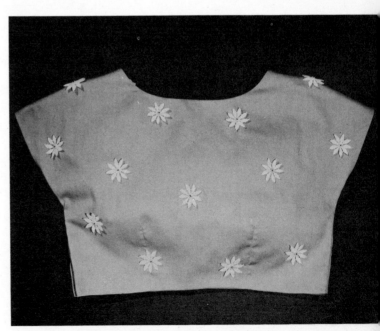

A. Sleeveless toppette trimmed in wide rickrack. (This one is double, but not reversible because of trim.)

B. Toppette with cut-on sleeve. (This one is double, but not reversible because of trim.) A small pearl button is sewn in the center of each daisy.

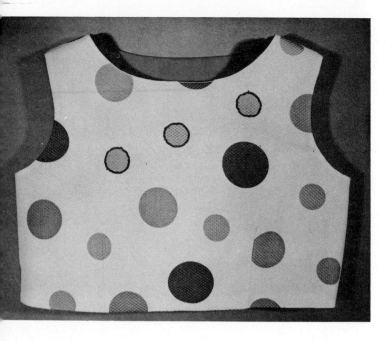

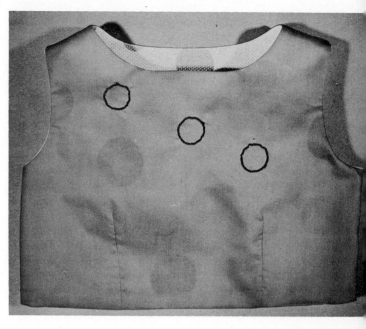

C. This is made of plain fabric on the underside, and is reversible.   Circles are stitched with zigzag stitch.

D. This is the reverse side of C.

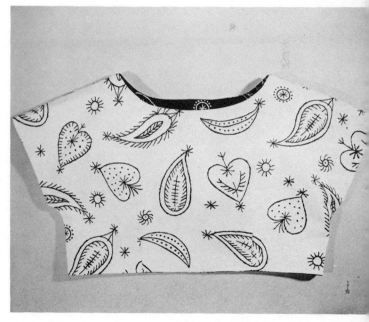

E. This is black fabric with a white print.

F. This is the reverse side of E, and is white fabric with a black print.   These are known as companion prints.

**Sleeveless toppette**

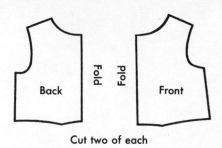

Cut two of each

Toppette A is cut 1¾" longer at center front
C and D are cut like pattern

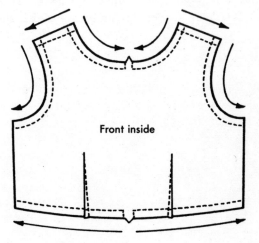

Front inside

**Front unit.** Staystitch neckline, shoulders, armholes, and lower edge just outside seamline, and in the direction arrows indicate. Stitch darts. Repeat these steps for the second front.

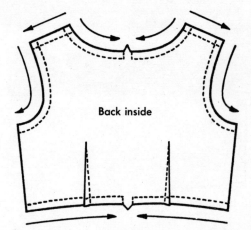

Back inside

**Back unit.** Staystitch neckline, shoulders, armholes, and lower edge just outside seamline, and in the direction arrows indicate. Stitch darts. Repeat these steps for the second back.

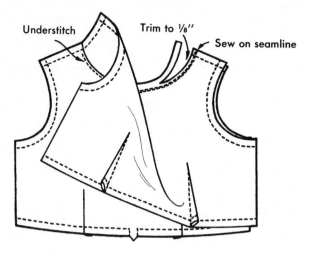

Underststitch  Trim to ⅛″  Sew on seamline

**Complete toppette unit.** With right sides together, sew one front to second front at neckline on seamline. Trim seam to ⅛ inch, and beginning and ending one inch from shoulder edge, understitch neckline.

As the photograph illustrates, to preserve the curve, work fabric up to needle in understitching this off-grain edge.

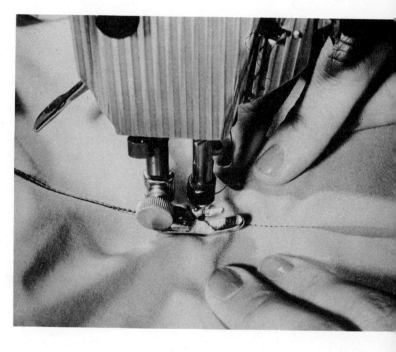

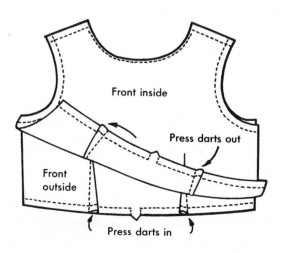

Front inside

Press darts out

Front outside

Press darts in

Turn fronts right side out, and press neckline. Press darts in one front toward center, and in second front toward side edge.

Repeat these same steps for the two backs of the toppette.

At armholes, right sides together, baste-stitch the second front to the first front for three inches down; lockstitch the threads; change length of machine stitch to a permanent one, and sew to side edge. Using an edge presser, press open baste-stitched areas of armholes. Trim the armhole seam to ⅛ inch. Remove baste-stitching and understitch lower part of armhole, ending one inch from side edge.

Repeat these same steps for the backs of the toppette.

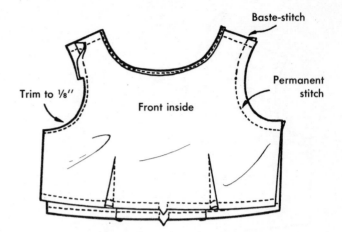

With right sides together, stitch first front to second front at lower edge on seamline. Trim seam to scant ¼ inch, and understitch, beginning and ending one inch from edge.

Repeat for backs of toppette.

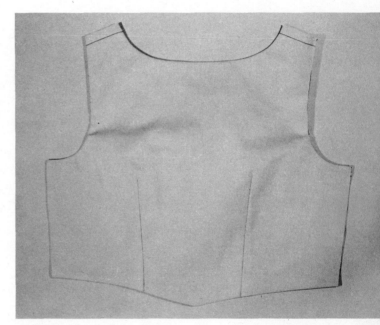

Turn backs wrong side out, and at the side seams, place right side of front toppette to right side of back toppette, and right side of front under section to right side of back under section. With a continuous line of stitching and a ⅝-inch seam, stitch a complete circle. Turn right side out after clipping seam to a point at armhole and lower edge. Press seam toward back of toppette (see this technique in photograph for vest, page 162).

Repeat for second side, except an opening must be left in the middle of underside to turn right side out. (See this step in photograph for vest, page 162.) Whipstitch these edges together.

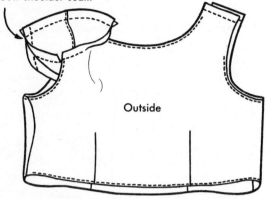

Sew shoulder seam

Outside

Closing the shoulder seams will now be a continuous operation with top and under section of toppette. On edge presser, press the seam open and trim to ¼ inch. Restore edges at neckline and armholes. Slipstitch the pressed armhole edges together.

Final-press toppette (Chapter 9, *The Bishop Method of Clothing Construction\**).

This toppette was not made with double construction because the sailcloth fabric was too heavy for that technique. It has a facing cut all in one for neckline and armholes, as you learned to do on pp. 35–36, *BMCC.*

\*This text will hereafter be referred to as *BMCC.*

# Lined toppettes for women and girls

**Toppette with cut-on sleeves**

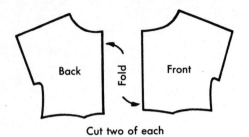

Cut two of each

**Back unit.** Make precisely like the front unit.

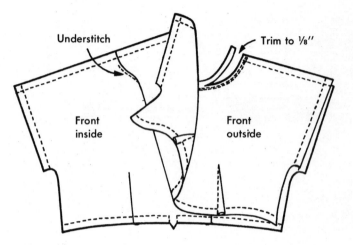

**Complete toppette unit.** With right sides together, sew one front to second front at neckline on seamline. Trim seam to ⅛ inch, and beginning and ending one inch from shoulder edge, understitch neckline. As the photograph on page 51 illustrates, to preserve the curve, work fabric up to needle in understitching this off grain edge.

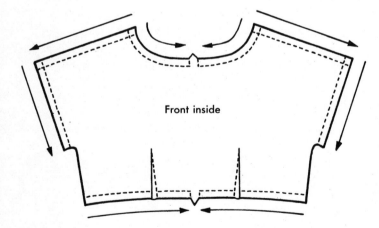

**Front unit.** Staystitch neckline, shoulders, sleeve edges, and lower edge just outside seamline, and in the direction arrows indicate. Stitch darts. Repeat these steps for the second front.

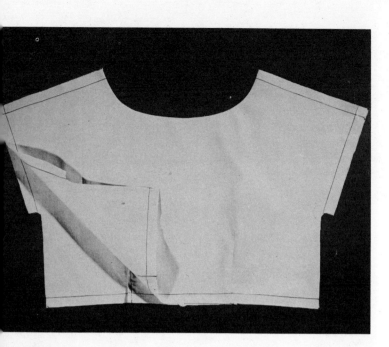

Turn fronts right side out, and press neckline. Press darts in one front toward center, and in second front toward underarm seam.

Repeat these same steps for the two backs of the overblouse.

Turn only the sleeve edges right sides together, and stitch sleeve edges on seamline. Trim seam to ⅛ inch, and understitch sleeve edges. Turn toppette right side out and press.

Closing the shoulder seams will now be a continuous operation with top and under section of overblouse. On edge presser, press the seam open, and trim to ¼ inch. Turn overblouse right side out and press shoulders.

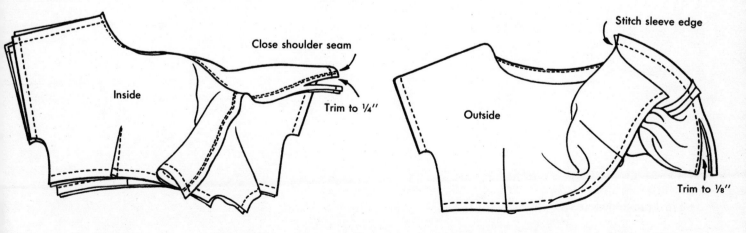

Inside

Close shoulder seam

Trim to ¼"

Stitch sleeve edge

Outside

Trim to ⅛"

## Lined toppettes for women and girls

This photograph shows sleeve edge (A) before it was completed, and (B) after it was completed.

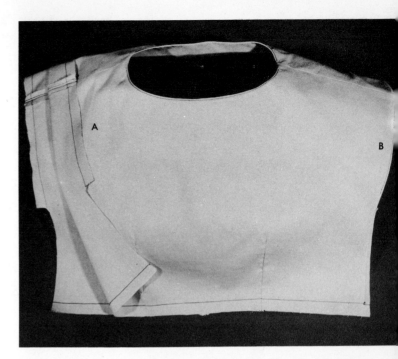

With right sides together, stitch lower edges of top and under sections of front toppette on seamline. Trim seam to ¼ inch and understitch (A).

Repeat these same steps for top and under sections of back toppette. Turn right side out and press lower edges of toppette.

At side edges, key together all four raw edges of fabric, and on the outside of toppette, stitch a ⅜-inch seam. Trim seam to a scant ⅛ inch and press together to one side. Turn to under sections and crease on stitched line. Stitch a scant ¼-inch seam from crease (B). Then, the seam may be stitched flat if the toppette is to be reversible.

Because of the cut-on sleeve, this style of toppette makes undesirable the technique that you used at the side seams of the sleeveless toppette (p. 52).

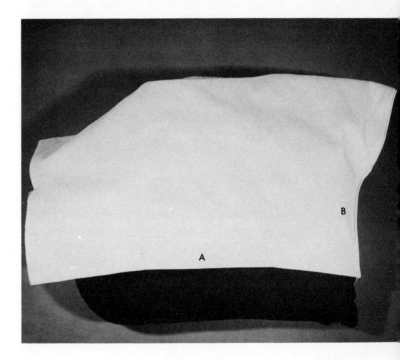

Final-press toppette (Chapter 9, *BMCC*).

# Chapter 6

# Robes from quilted fabrics for women and girls

A robe from quilted cotton fabric will be cut and made in a different manner than a robe from any of the quilted synthetic fabrics because of the various characteristics of the fabrics. We are going to show the techniques on two robes for little girls, but they will be unchanged for all robes for young and old alike.

As we have said of children's dresses, not only do we want you to be able to turn out quality-looking robes, but we want them to be strong and durable for the hard wearings and many launderings they will receive.

Mother and daughter robes are always a family joy.

Before cutting out a robe, read the section of the chapter for the kind of quilted fabric you are using.

**Basic learnings for a robe from quilted cotton fabric**

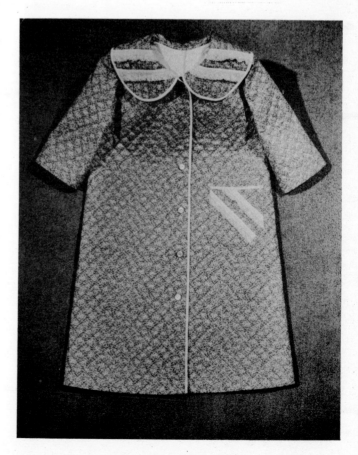

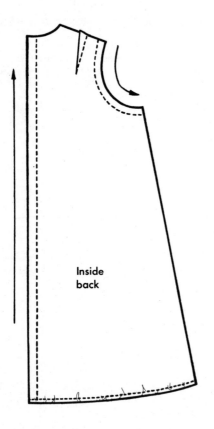

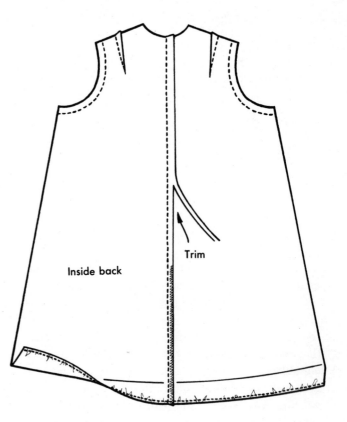

**Back unit.** Staystich armholes just outside seam-line and in direction arrows indicate. The quilting helps to control the cut edges of the fabric, so it will not be necessary to staystitch any other edges.

Staystitch-plus lower edge (middle photo, page 46, *The Bishop Method of Clothing Construction*°) ¼ inch from edge to prepare for hemming. With quilted fabric, use a short stitch at machine, and press finger as firmly as possible against the back of the presser foot to be certain of drawing up fabric as much as needed. If you ever draw it up too much, it is very easy to hold fabric firm and loosen after pressing hem. Stitch center back seam in direction shown, and stitch neckline darts.

Press center back seam to one side and neckline darts toward center back. Using hem gauge, turn up hem 1½ inches and press. Trim center back seam to ⅜ inch and zigzag edges together in same direction seam was sewn.

If you do not have a zigzag machine, a special attachment, called overcaster, is available for popular makes of straight-stitch machines. Or, you may choose to bind the seams as we will show on the front edges and around the collar. Do not trim any of the seam to the fold of the hem (see page 142, *BMCC*) in children's clothes because of the need to lengthen them.

°This text will hereafter be referred to as *BMCC*.

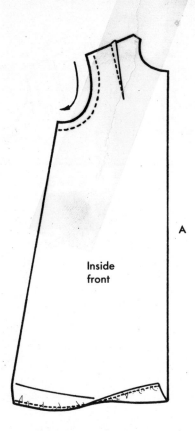

Inside
front

A

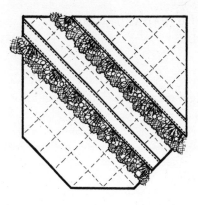

**Pocket unit.** In the Bishop method, we have repeatedly tried to instill the idea that *the fabric should tell you what to do* for a trimming detail on a garment. For this pocket, lace was gathered (see collar for instructions) and placed under edge of bias. Then, the bias was stitched flat at the machine, *following the design of the quilted fabric.* The top edge was bound (see collar for instructions) and the raw edges were pressed under ½ inch to form an attractively shaped pocket using the quilted design.

**Front unit.** A front facing is not recommended on the quilted cotton fabric. Trim away seam allowance at edge A (may be done to pattern before cutting out robe) to prepare edge for binding.

Staystitch armholes just outside seamline and in direction arrows indicate. Staystitch-plus lower edge same as back unit to prepare for hemming. Stitch neckline dart and press toward center front. Using hem gauge, turn up hem 1½ inches and press.

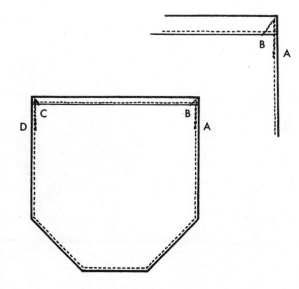

For added strength, make topstitching double at top of pocket. Begin topstitching at A, go up to B, turn robe and stitch all around pocket to C; turn robe again and complete stitching at D.

59

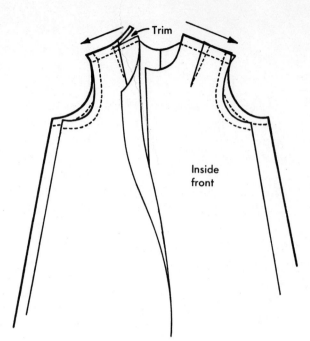

**Complete robe unit.** Stitch shoulder seams in direction shown, and press toward back. Trim to ⅜ inch, and zigzag in same direction as seams were stitched.

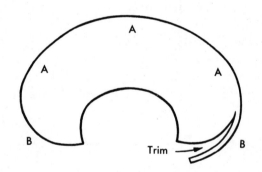

**Collar unit.** Trim away ⅝-inch seam allowance from outside edge (A) of collar to prepare for binding. If collar pattern has points at outer edges (B), round off for ease in binding.

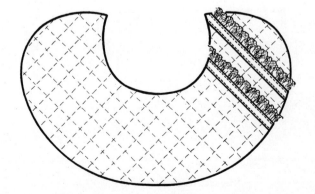

The trimming on the collar is a repeat performance of the pocket. Cut 1½ times the needed length of lace (for example, if you need 6 inches length, cut 9 inches), and gather by pulling a thread that is woven along the inside edge of lace. (See sketch on page 67.) Place lace under edge of bias, and stitch bias flat at machine.

Collar is always made singly in quilted fabric. Open up folded bias, and key raw edge of bias to raw edge of under collar. Stitch in fold of bias ¼ inch from edge on underside of collar. Turn bias to top of collar, and topstitch along second folded edge. Where and if necessary, trim away fraction of quilted fabric, so bias tape can lie smoothly for topstitching.

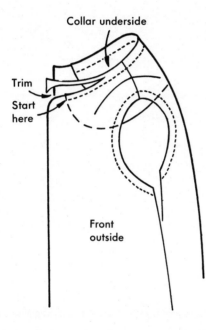

Place outside edge of collar to inside of robe. Key edges of collar to center fronts of robe, and center back of collar to center back of robe. With garment side up, stitch collar to robe in ⅝-inch seam. Trim collar and neckline seam to ¼ inch, rounding off corners to nothing at front edges.

At A and B, turn in raw edges of bias ¼ inch and beginning at one lower front edge of robe and continuing around neckline to second lower front edge, stitch bias tape to underside of robe, same as collar edge. Turn bias to top of robe and topstitch along second folded edge. Where and if necessary, trim away fraction of quilted fabric so that bias tape can lie smoothly for topstitching. Keep fabric to left of needle for topstitching.

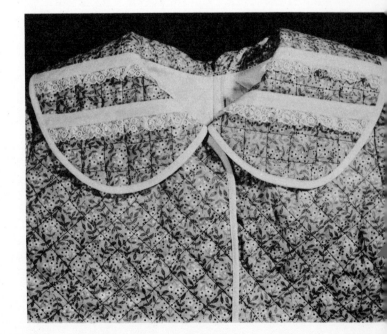

Turn folded edge of bias (A) to lie flat on underside of collar. Stitch along folded edge of bias for added support (B) and smooth, flat finish on under collar.

This is the finished collar.

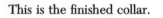

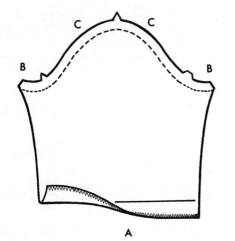

**Sleeve and side seam unit.**  Zigzag lower edge (A) of sleeve.  Precisely on ⅝-inch seamline, stay-stitch cap of sleeve (B and B), changing to longest stitch (C) between notches.

Using hem gauge, turn up hem 1½ inches and press.

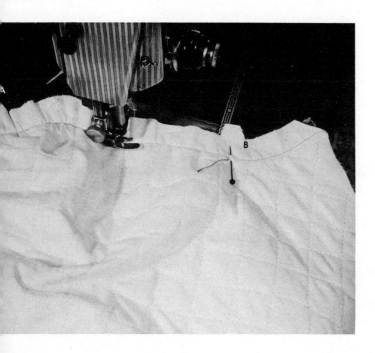

With right sides together, pin notch at top of sleeve (A) to shoulder seam of robe.  To prepare the sleeve to sew in the armhole, clip the first long stitch at the notch on the right side of the inside of the sleeve (B). Draw up that side of sleeve cap slightly to fit that half of the armhole.  Clip the first long stitch at the notch on the left side of the inside of the sleeve, and draw up second half of sleeve cap slightly to fit second half of armhole.  With sleeve side up, stitch sleeve to arm-hole of robe, sewing one thread inside line of stay-stitching and ease line.  Trim seam to ⅜ inch, and with sleeve side down, zigzag at machine.  Do not press (see photo, p. 70).

The sleeve and side seams of quilted robes are al-ways stitched in one operation.  Stitch from bottom up (see photo, p. 70), and press toward back of robe. Trim to ⅜ inch, and zigzag together at machine from bottom up.

Hem sleeves at machine like bottom photograph, page 46, *BMCC*.

**Hem unit.** Press and restore hem lines at side seams of robe. Zigzag lower edge, and hem robe at machine. To hem by machine, fold the hem under as shown. Take 4 or 5 stitches along the underside of the hem. Then take 1 stitch into fold of the garment. Continue around entire hem.

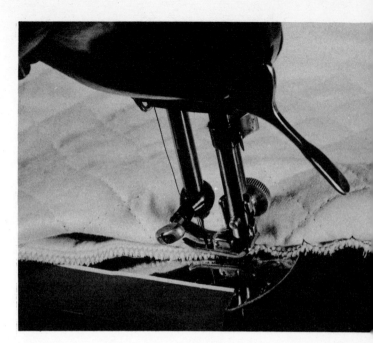

At front edge of robe, stitch hem firmly just inside bias tape.

Outside

Stitch

**Complete robe unit.** Make buttonholes and sew on buttons (page 84, *BMCC*). A small button on underside (A) is sewn with top button (B) for support to the single layer of fabric.

Final-press robe (Chapter 9, *BMCC*).

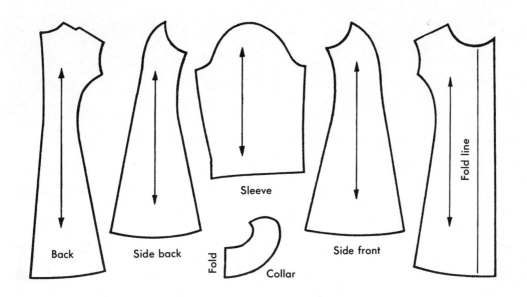

Back      Side back      Fold    Sleeve      Collar      Side front      Fold line

## Basic learnings for a robe from quilted synthetic fabric

**Back unit.** Staystitch armholes of back and side back just outside seamline and in direction arrows indicate. The quilting helps to control the cut edges of the fabric; so it will not be necessary to staytitch any other edges.

Staystitch-plus lower edges (page 46, *BMCC*) ¼ inch from edge to prepare for hemming. With quilted fabric, use a short stitch at machine and press finger as firmly as possible against the back of the presser foot to be certain of drawing up fabric as much as needed. If you ever draw it up too much, it is very easy to hold fabric firm and loosen after pressing hem. Using hem gauge, turn up hem 1½ inches and press.

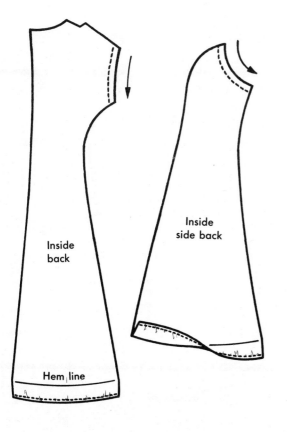

Inside back      Inside side back      Hem line

**65**

Stitch center back seam in direction shown, and stitch neckline darts. When attempting to stitch seams to come out thread perfect in this thick and slippery fabric, it will help to hold the under layer firm with your right hand. Stitch back of robe to side back, keeping *inside* curve on top. On right back seam, begin at bottom of robe, and keeping inside curve on top, stitch all the way to the armhole. On left back seam, stitch from bottom of robe to waistline for correct direction of grain. Then, turn and stitch from armhole to waistline with inside curve on top. On quilted fabric, you will have to clip the inside curve toward the seamline for stitching, because it does not give.

Press neckline darts to center back, press center back seam to one side, and press side back seams toward side edges. Trim seams to ⅜ inch and zigzag edges together in the same direction they were sewn. If you do not have a zigzag machine, a special attachment, called overcaster, is available for popular makes of straight-stitch machines. Or, you may choose to bind the seams with rayon or nylon bias tape as we have shown on page 61. Do not trim any of the seam to the fold of the hem (see page 142, *BMCC*) in children's clothes, because of the need to lengthen them.

**Front unit.** A cut-on-facing is more desirable than a separate one with quilted synthetic fabric. If pattern has a separate facing, pin tissue together and cut as one.

To press, proceed as follows: Mark one layer of fabric only (A) with tracing paper and wheel. Through both layers of fabric, place 3 or 4 pins in marking line. Turn back and press top layer on pin line (see photographs, page 164). Remove pins. Turn fabric to have under layer on top. Fold back top layer to meet under fold and press second side.

Staystitch armholes just outside seamline and in direction arrows indicate. Staystitch-plus lower edge same as back unit to prepare for hemming. Using hem gauge, turn up hem 1½ inches and press.

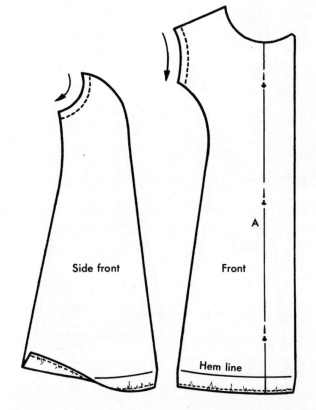

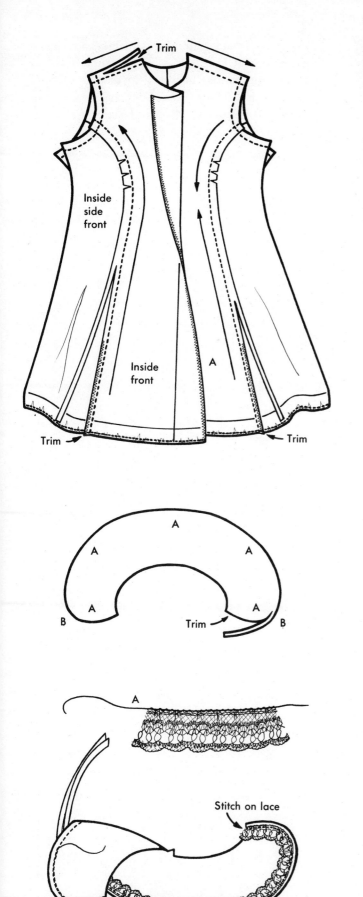

Stitch front of robe to side front, keeping *inside* curve on top, with the same techniques you learned on the back unit. On quilted fabric, you will have to clip the inside curve toward the seamline for stitching, because it does not give. Press seams toward side edges, trim to ⅜ inch, and zigzag edges together in the same direction they were sewn. Next, zigzag edges of facings (A).

Stitch shoulder seams in direction shown, and press toward back. Trim to ⅜ inch, and zigzag in same direction as seams were stitched.

**Collar unit.** Trim away ½ inch of the ⅝-inch seam allowance from outside edge (A) of collar to prepare for binding (remaining ⅛ inch will be trimmed later). If collar pattern has points at outer edges (B), round off for ease in binding. Cut 1½ times the needed length of lace for A edge (for example, if A measures 20 inches, cut 30 inches of lace).

Gather lace by pulling a thread that is woven along the inside edge of it (A).

Stitch lace on collar ¼ inch from raw edge. Open out folded, commercial bias and right sides together, place raw edge along raw edge of collar. Turn to underside of collar and stitch on bias through row of previous stitching. Trim ¼-inch seam to ⅛ inch.

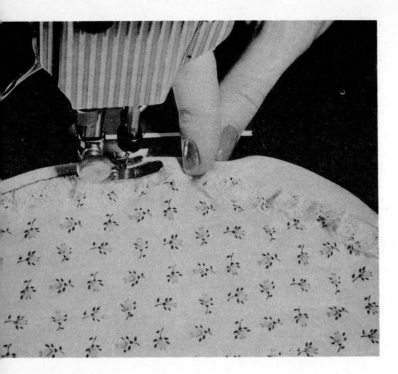

Turn bias to underside over cut edge, and without pressing it, stitch bias in place through seamline groove on topside. Collar is always made singly in quilted fabric. This lace trim is more unusual, attractive, and durable than having the lace turn toward the outside of the collar.

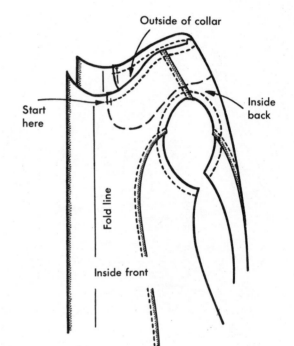

To put on collar, place underside of collar to outside of robe; key and pin outside edges of collar to center fronts of robe, and center back of collar to center back of robe. With garment side up, stitch collar to robe with ⅝-inch seam.

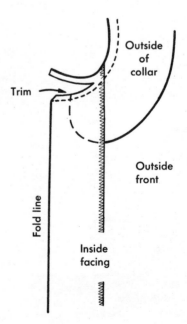

Then, turn facings to outside of robe on fold line, and again with garment side up, sew on facings through previous stitching to end of facings. Trim entire collar seam to ¼ inch.

Open out folded, commercial bias, and with right sides together, place raw edge along raw edge of collar; overlap on facings for one inch (A). With garment side up, sew on bias through previous stitching.

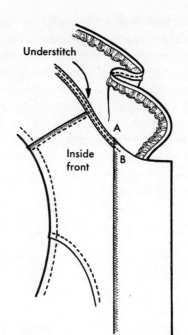

Understitch

Inside front

A

B

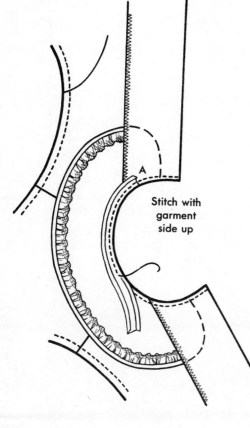

Stitch with garment side up

A

Turn facings to inside and understitch neck edge of bias (A). Then, stitch bias flat to robe, beginning and ending stitching ½ inch over edge of facings (B).

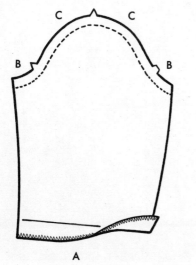

C     C

B     B

A

**Sleeve and side-seam unit.** Zigzag lower edge (A) of sleeve. Precisely on ⅝-inch seamline, staystitch cap of sleeve (B and B), changing to longest stitch (C) between notches.

Using hem gauge, turn up hem 1½ inches and press.

With right sides together, pin notch at top of sleeve to shoulder seam of robe. To prepare the sleeve to sew in the armhole, clip the first long stitch at the notch on the right side of the inside of the sleeve. Draw up that side of sleeve cap slightly to fit that half of the armhole. Clip the first long stitch at the notch on the left side of the inside of the sleeve, and draw up second half of sleeve cap slightly to fit second half of armhole. With sleeve side up, stitch sleeve to armhole of robe, sewing one thread inside line of staystitching and ease line.

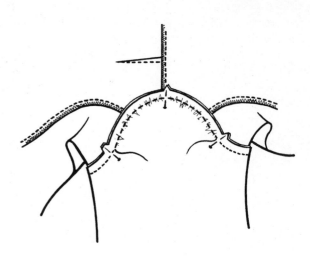

Trim seam to ⅜ inch, and with sleeve side down, zigzag at machine. Do not press.

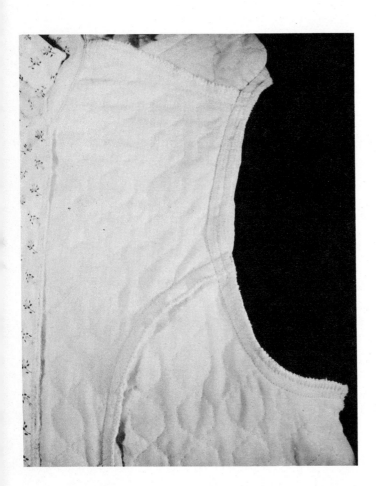

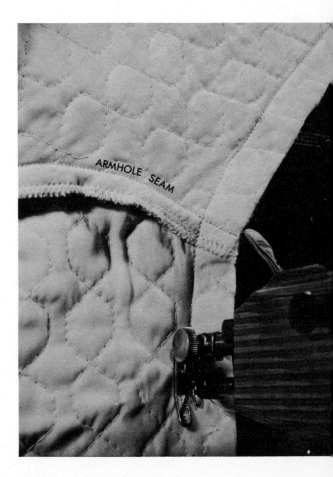

The sleeve and side seams of quilted robes are always stitched in one operation. Stitch from bottom up, and press seam toward front of robe, opposite of elbow ease, or possible elbow dart on pattern. Trim to ⅜ inch and zigzag together at machine from bottom up.

Hem sleeves at machine like bottom photograph, page 46, *BMCC*.

**Hem unit.** Press and restore hem lines at seams of robes. Zigzag lower edge.

Turn back facings and stitch hem of facings to hem of robe ¼ inch from edge.

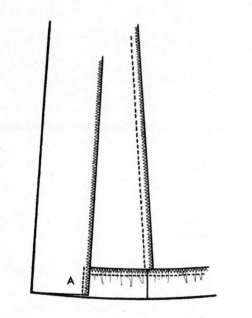

Turn facings to inside again, and stitch edge of facing to hem (A).

Hem robe at machine like bottom photograph, page 46, *BMCC*.

**Complete robe unit.** Make buttonholes and sew on buttons (pages 84–85, *BMCC*).

Final-press robe (Chapter 9, *BMCC*).

# Chapter 7

# Robes for men and boys

What a pleasant surprise it would be for your favorite men and boys to receive a robe you made for them personally. As you study the chapter, you will see that many fine techniques have been developed for making them. You will have fun in making robes, also. Popular fabrics are cotton broadcloth, cotton plaid, terry cloth, cotton or silk surah, seersucker, corduroy, or wool challis. The collar and cuffs may be in contrast, if desired.

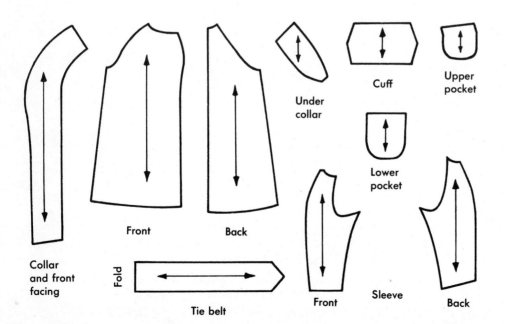

Collar and front facing

Fold

Tie belt

Front

Back

Under collar

Cuff

Upper pocket

Lower pocket

Front   Sleeve   Back

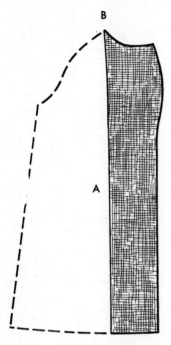

Front interfacing

### Interfacing unit

Cut the interfacing from robe front pattern the width of facing pattern at A, tapering to edge of neckline at B.

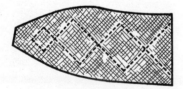

Collar interfacing

Use the under collar pattern and cut the interfacing on identical grain of under collar.

With tracing paper and tracing wheel, mark a stitching pattern for stitching interfacing to under collar. It can form various designs, providing lines are on crosswise and lengthwise threads of interfacing.

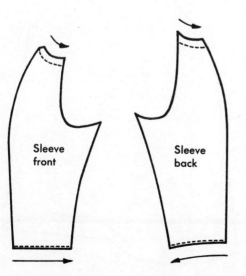

Sleeve front

Sleeve back

### Sleeve unit

Staystitch neck edge of sleeve in direction shown, just outside seamline, and lower edge ¼ inch from edge.

Wrong sides together, sew sleeve back to sleeve front on seamline in direction shown.

Press seam toward sleeve front. Trim the lower seam allowance to ⅛ or ¼ inch; turn under raw edge of upper seam allowance, and stitch flat to garment in a flat-felled seam.

In plain fabric, the flat-felled seam is always finished from the topside of the garment, and the two rows of stitching give added interest.

However, if the fabric has surface interest, the flat-felled seam may be finished on the underside, and only one row of stitching will show on the topside.

With silk fabrics, use a French seam.

French and flat-felled seams are illustrated on page 120, *The Bishop Method of Clothing Construction.*\*

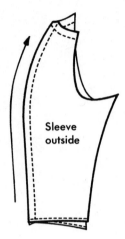

Sleeve outside

## Back unit

Staystitch neckline in direction shown, just outside seamline, and lower edge ¼ inch from edge.

Turn under and press raw edge on staystitching ¼ inch from edge, and turn up hem desired amount. Press with hem gauge, shown on page 3, *BMCC*. Hem back unit like bottom photograph, page 45, *BMCC*.

However, in a cotton robe, the hem may just be topstitched to robe at machine.

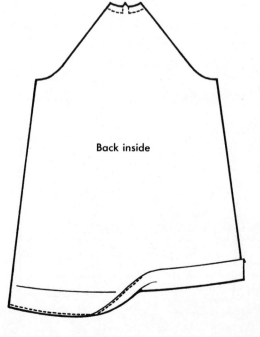

Back inside

---

\*This text will be hereafter referred to as *BMCC*.

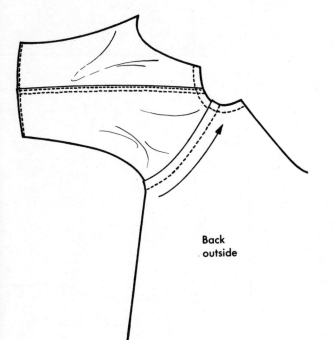

**Back outside**

Wrong sides together, sew sleeve back to robe back on seamline in direction shown.

Press seam toward sleeve and finish with a flat-felled seam, the same as you learned to do in the sleeve unit. Repeat for second sleeve.

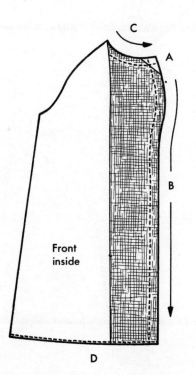

**Front inside**

### Front unit

Place interfacing on underside of robe front. At corner A, trim interfacing out of seamline (page 173, *BMCC*). Staystitch edge B on seamline in direction shown, edge C just outside seamline, and lower edge D ¼ inch from edge.

Turn under and press lower edge on staystitching ¼ inch from edge. Turn up hem desired amount and press with hem gauge.

## Pocket unit

The pockets are made and stitched to robe precisely like the instructions on page 121, *BMCC*.

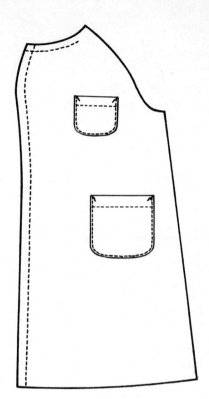

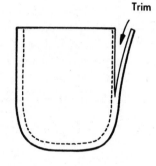

However, if the pocket has a curved lower edge, staystitch curved edge on seamline; trim seam to ¼ inch. Turn and press curved edge on staystitching on seamline before topstitching pocket to robe.

The letters on the pocket in the photograph at the beginning of this chapter were white, and were hand sewn to pocket with red embroidery floss.

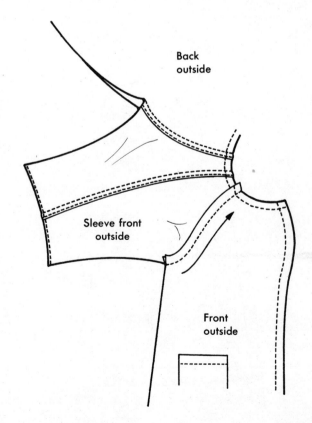

## Complete robe unit

Wrong sides together, sew sleeve front to robe front on seamline in direction shown.

Press seam toward sleeve and finish with a flat-felled seam, the same as you learned to do in the sleeve unit. Repeat for second sleeve.

## Collar unit

At corners marked with A, cut away interfacing diagonally ¼ inch beyond seamline. Place interfacing with under collar, and staystitch B edges on seamline and C edges just outside seamline in direction shown.

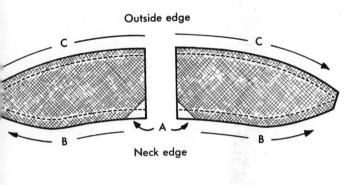

Outside edge

Neck edge

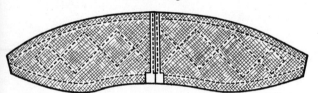

Outside edge

Neck edge

Inside

Stitch center back seam of under collar and interfacing and press open. Trim away interfacing up to seamline. Topstitch each side of seam, beginning at neck edge and continuing down one side to ¾ inch from outside edge. Cross over to other side and topstitch up to neck edge. Trim under collar seam to topstitching, except lower edge that is not topstitched.

The stitching pattern is drawn on *exact grain* of interfacing. Stitch on stitching pattern through interfacing and under collar. Do not sew beyond staystitching.

Right sides together, key center back of under collar to center back of robe. With robe side up, stitch collar to robe in a ⅝-inch seam.

Clip robe seam at two shoulder seams (marked with A), and press open seams up to clipping. Across the back of the robe, press the seam toward the collar. Trim interfacing out of entire seam to seamline, and trim seam across back of robe to ¼ inch.

Topstitch both sides of seam up to clipping at shoulder seam; trim seam to topstitching.

## Facing unit

Right sides together, sew facing at center back on seamline. Press open seam and trim to ¼ inch.

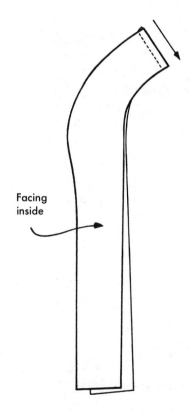

Facing inside

Right sides together, and with robe side up, sew facings to robe through staystitching on seamline of robe and under collar.   At outer edge, trim center back seam of under collar to ⅛ inch.

Trim interfacing to seamline and robe seam to ¼ inch.   In heavier fabrics, stagger width of robe seam as you have learned on page 161, *BMCC*. It is not necessary to reverse widths in staggering at the turn of the lapel in a robe.

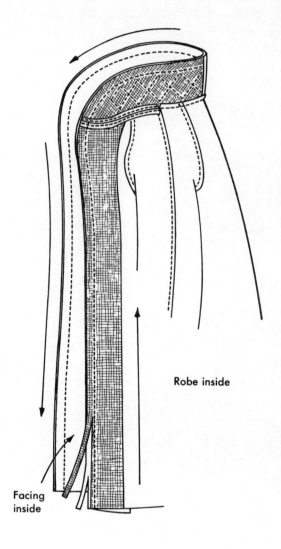

Robe inside

Facing
inside

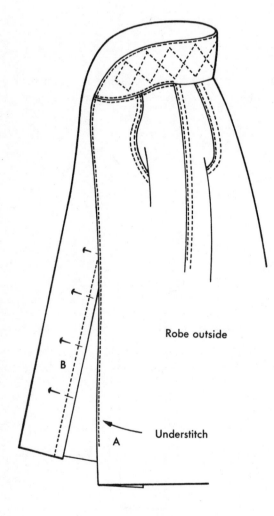

Robe outside

Understitch

A

B

Beginning and ending above the top of the hemline (A), understitch robe.   The understitching will be on the underside of the collar and lapels, but will be on the top of the robe for remainder of robe front below lapels.

Press this edge with perfection; then, pin edge of facing to edge of interfacing (B).   Staystitch together ⅝ inch from edge, and trim away interfacing to staystitching.

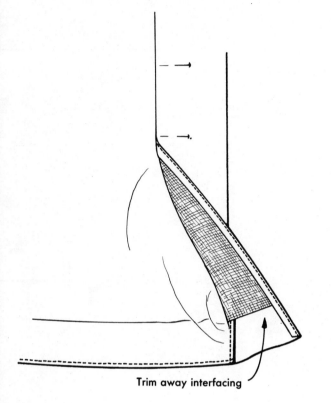

Trim away interfacing

Press under seam allowance on facing up to stay-stitching and pin flat to robe.

Restore hemline at lower edge of robe. Trim away interfacing a little beyond depth of hem.

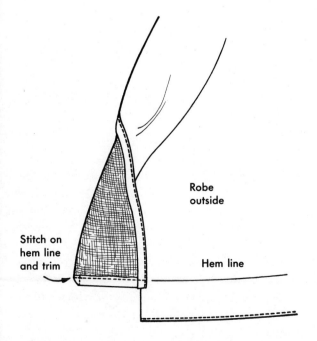

Robe
outside

Stitch on
hem line
and trim

Hem line

Turn facing to outside of robe and stitch on hem-line. Trim away hem allowance to ¼ inch; turn right side out and press.

Finish hem same as back unit. Then, stitch the facing to the robe at the machine, going all around the facing continuously from lower edge A to the same place on the opposite side.

This photograph shows the facing as it forms the top collar. It is stitched to the inside of the robe at the machine.

## Complete robe unit

Make a strip of bias for belt loops as you learned to do on page 193, *BMCC*.

Stitch in place at waistline, keying raw edges of loops to raw edges of back side-seam edge on both sides of robe back.

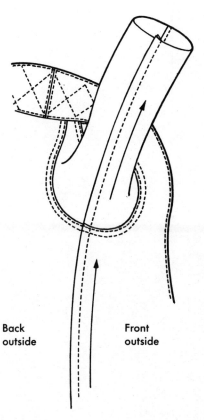

Back
outside

Wrong sides together, sew side seams of robe and sleeves on seamline from bottom up. Press seam toward back of robe and finish with a flat-felled seam the same as you learned to do in the sleeve unit.

Back
outside

Front
outside

Right sides together, stitch a ¼-inch seam on belt, leaving an opening in the middle of the belt at the seamline to turn right side out. Trim corners, turn, and press. Slipstitch opening by hand.

Fasten belt to robe with a second piece of bias (A) that is placed through belt loop (B). Anchor-stitch piece of bias to belt at C and D. The belt has some give, but being attached it will never fall off the robe.

## Cuff unit

Right sides together, sew cuff seam on seamline. Press open seam, trim to ¼ inch, and turn right side out.

Staystitch A and B edges together (shown in previous sketch) ¼ inch from edge.

Place right side of cuff to wrong side of sleeve. Sew cuff to sleeve on seamline, and finish with a flat-felled seam exactly as you learned to do on page 107, *BMCC*.

Final-press robe, Chapter 9, *BMCC*.

# Chapter 8

# Children's dresses

A good deal of time and research has gone into the preparation of this chapter. Not only did we want you to be able to turn out quality-looking dresses, but we wanted the dresses to be strong and durable for the hard wearings and many launderings they will receive. The constant mending with a stitch here and there at the end of every laundering has been eliminated. We have used techniques, such as the finishes on the lower edges of the sleeves of the two dresses, that will make them easy to iron, also.

We will make two dresses in this chapter to cover all the techniques we want to present, but certainly you could combine and use some of the techniques from both dresses that would be desirable for the style and fabric you were using. It is worthy of note that there is still a continuing trend of mother and daughter fashions.

Remember that your daughter depends on you to teach her how to dress. She should be dressed with care, with sufficient attention paid to details, but without overemphasis on looks and clothes.

A child's clothing should reflect childhood—with gay colors, amusing touches now and then, but with simplicity. Colors should be becoming to hair, eyes, and skin coloring, and should coordinate well. Linens, broadcloths, fine cottons, and other simple fabrics are preferred to the overdone varieties.

To determine the pattern size for children's dresses, take a chest measurement, the same as the high bust measurement is taken for women. If necessary, pattern alterations are also made before cutting out dress. For example, the bodice would be lengthened or shortened the same as it would be done for women.

In purchasing fabric for children's dresses, it is most important to buy prints that are printed on grain, because the off-grain design would show when the strips are torn for the gathered skirt. Plain, dark cottons do not hold up as well in laundering as a small dot, check, or print. Then, unless it is removable, a white trim on a dark dress (such as a white collar) is not desirable.

Read the entire chapter before cutting dress.

Children's coats are made with the same techniques shown for women's coats in Chapter 11, *The Bishop Method of Clothing Construction.**

**Basic learnings for a dress without underlining bodice**

---

*Referred to hereafter as *BMCC*.

## Children's dresses

**Skirt unit.** Determine length to tear strips by the height of the child and desired width of hem. This first dress is a size 8 in a softer fabric, and the hem is 8½ inches deep. The dress to follow is a size 6 and the hem is 3½ inches deep. A deeper hem gives more character and better quality to the skirt.

Always tear the strips for a gathered skirt and always tear them to hang lengthwise. If desired, the top of the dress can be cut crosswise in a stripe, etc., but never the skirt for a quality look. If you buy a border print, the skirt should be pleated instead of gathered, because fabric does not gather gracefully on the lengthwise edge. Both dresses have 3 widths of fabric in the skirt, although a smaller size would only be 2 widths. This dress was made from fabric 45 inches wide, and the next dress was made from fabric 36 inches wide.

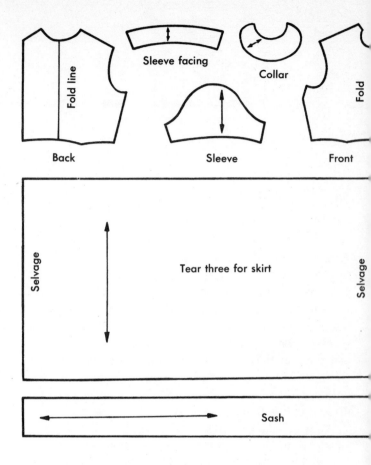

In both books, we have tried to stress that one of your keys to success is the preparation of your fabric to grain perfection. Press the torn strips with the iron to restore the grain on the torn edges, and also to assure that the skirt pieces lie grain perfect when folded in half.

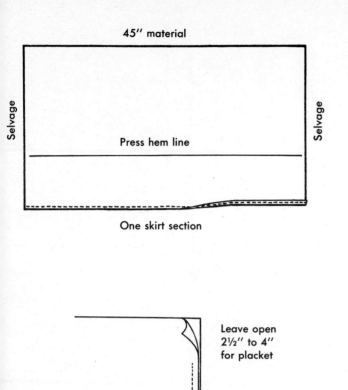

45" material

Selvage

Press hem line

Selvage

One skirt section

Staystitch each skirt section ¼ inch from lower edge. Then, using hem gauge, turn up hem to correct finished length and press. Next, turn under raw edge ¼ inch on staystitching and press.

Leave open
2½" to 4"
for placket

Skirt
sections

Open out hem and stitch seams of skirt ⅜ inch wide, leaving one of them open at top of skirt for 2½ to 4 inches for placket opening at center back.

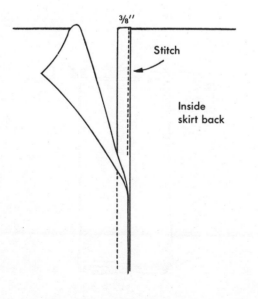

⅜"

Stitch

Inside
skirt back

On left side of center back opening, turn in ⅜-inch seam allowance, press, and stitch near edge of selvage.

On right side of center back opening, turn in ¾ inch, press, and stitch near edge of selvage.

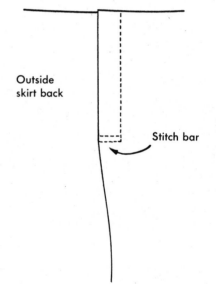

Lap right side of opening over left one, and stitch a bar at lower edge to hold opening securely. This technique is similar to the placket opening for shirts, page 108, *BMCC*.

Press open skirt seams and restore hem lines. Hem dress at machine as in bottom photograph, page 46, *BMCC*.

Beginning at center back, fold skirt in 4 sections. Snip with scissors to identify center front and 2 sides. This division will place more gathers in the back of the skirt than the front, as it should be, since the front bodice is cut wider than the back.

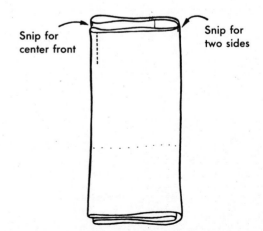

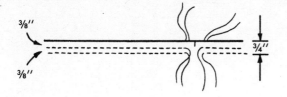

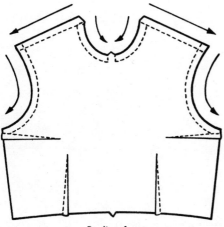

Outside skirt

Make gathers in 4 sections with longest stitch at machine. The first row will be ⅜ inch from raw edge, and second row ⅜ inch from first row (or ¾ inch from raw edge). You may find that using the attachment for gathering is very satisfactory if you can control the amount of gathers to fit the bodice.

Bodice front

**Bodice front unit.** Staystitch neckline, shoulders, and armholes just outside seamline, and in direction arrows indicate. Stitch darts (page 27, *BMCC*), and press bust darts toward waistline, and waistline darts toward center front.

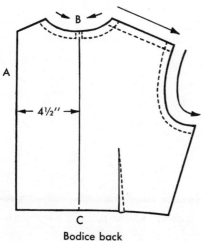

Bodice back

**Bodice back unit.** It is preferable to have facing cut in one with bodice back, and to have A edge on the selvage. Make facing wide for support; on this size 8 dress, we cut it 4½ inches wide.

Clip fold line for facing for ⅛ inch at B and C. Turn facings to inside at clips and press in place on fold line.

Staystitch neckline, shoulders, and armholes just outside seamline, and in direction arrows indicate. Stitch waistline darts and press toward center back.

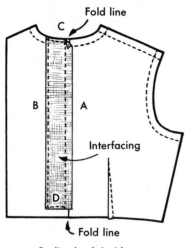

Fold line

C

B    A

Interfacing

D

Fold line

Bodice back inside

Tear a lengthwise strip of interfacing the length of bodice and 1½ to 2 inches wide to reinforce opening for buttons and buttonholes. Place it toward back of bodice (A) ⅛ inch beyond fold line, but stitch in place on facing side ⅛ inch from fold. Stitch ⅛ inch from second edge of facing (B) and neckline (C). Stitch ⅝ inch from lower edge (D), and trim away interfacing up to stitching.

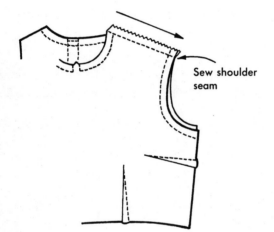

Sew shoulder seam

Stitch shoulder seams in direction arrows indicate, and pink with pinking shears.

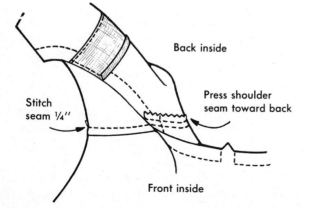

Back inside

Press shoulder seam toward back

Stitch seam ¼″

Front inside

Press toward back of bodice. Stitch seam ¼ inch from shoulder seamline to hold in place on back of bodice.

**Collar unit.** Make enough bias cording for collar, sleeves, and front of waistline seam. If the dress does not have a sash, bias cording is used around entire waistline seam. Cut true bias one inch wide (page 193, *BMCC*). Use a very fine cable cord, or a very heavy string, and fold bias over cord. Stitch close to cord with left side of zipper foot. For collar only, trim seam to perfect ¼ inch beyond stitching line. It is much easier to manage stitching cording on curved collar with a narrow seamline.

Trim away ⅝ inch from outside edge of top and under collar. ⅜ inch is the difference in seam allowance given by the commercial pattern that you will not be using, and the ¼ inch is the amount collar will be larger than original pattern with bias cording extending on finished collar.

Place raw edges of bias to meet raw edges of *top* collar. Clip seamline of cording around curves of collar. Using left side of zipper foot, stitch through same line of previous stitching on cording.

With right sides together, and with short stitches at machine, sew under collar to top collar. Keep top collar side turned up, and sew through stitching on top collar, again with zipper foot.

Trim all of seam to scant ⅛ inch; turn, and press.

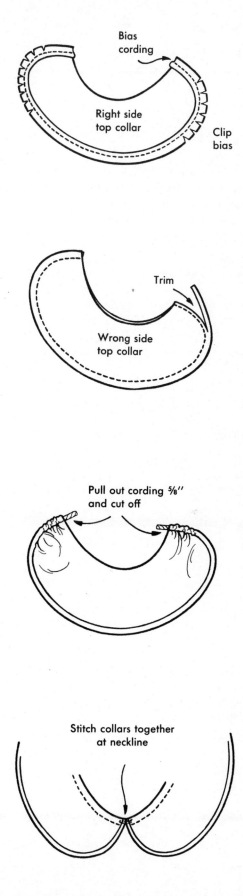

At each end of collar, pull cording out ⅝ inch and cut off.

Then, restore shape of collar. At neckline, stitch together top and under collar just outside seamline. Key the two collars precisely and overstitch about 1 inch to hold together so that they will not slip or spread when attached to the center front of bodice.

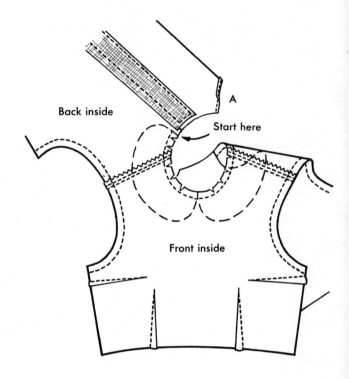

Place collar in position at center front and center back, and with dress side up, stitch collar to dress with ⅝-inch seam allowance. Clip curve of dress and collar frequently up to seamline to straighten curve for ease in stitching.

Staystitch shoulder edge of facing (A) ⅛ inch from edge, and turn in raw edge on staystitching to clean-finish.

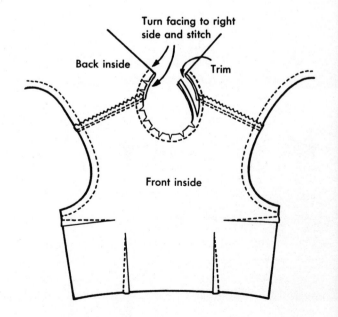

Turn facings to right side of dress on fold line, and stitch in place at neckline with dress side up. Trim entire neckline seam to *scant* ¼ inch.

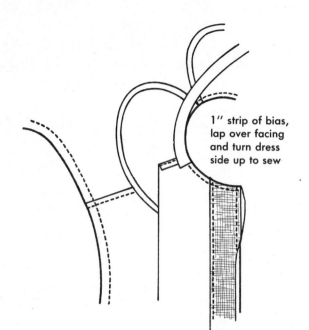

1" strip of bias, lap over facing and turn dress side up to sew

Cut a piece of bias one inch wide and lap over facings ¼ inch. With dress side up, sew on bias through previous stitching.

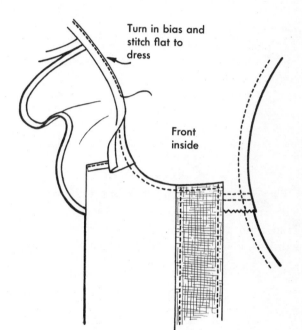

Turn in bias and stitch flat to dress

Front inside

If necessary, trim width of bias, so it will just turn in a narrow amount and fit over scant ¼-inch seam. Stitch flat to dress.

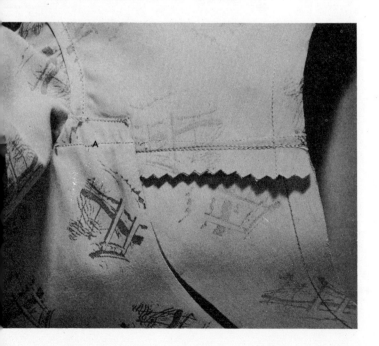

Turn facings to inside of dress. Then, for added strength, and with dress side up, stitch back facing in well of shoulder seamline (A). Press finished neckline. We have eliminated the front facing at the neckline for ease in ironing.

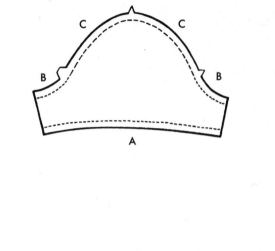

**Sleeve unit.** Staystitch lower edge A, just outside seamline. Precisely on ⅝-inch seamline, staystitch cap of sleeve (B and B), changing to longest stitch at machine (C) between notches.

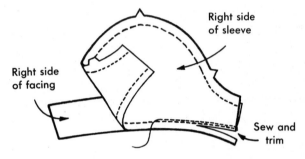

Place right side of facing to underside of sleeve, and with sleeve side up, sew facing to sleeve on seamline. Trim seam to scant ¼ inch. Understitch seam, beginning and ending one inch from edge. Turn facing to top of sleeve and press in place.

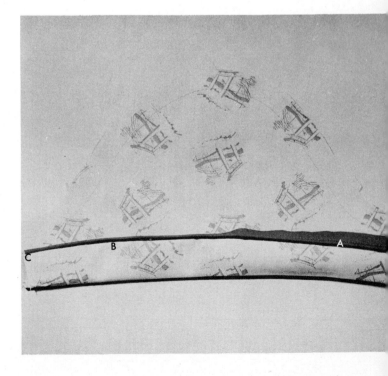

Trim seam of cording to perfect ¼ inch beyond stitching line. Trim away ⅜ of ⅝-inch seam allowance at top of facing. It is always easier to reduce seam when sewing in bias cording.

Place raw edges of bias to meet raw edge of facing. Using left side of zipper foot, stitch through same line of previous stitching on cording (A). Place facing in position on sleeve, press, and stitch facing to sleeve in well of cording seamline (B). At each end of sleeve, pull cording out ⅝ inch and cut off (C and C). Then, restore shape of sleeve.

To prepare sleeve to set in armhole, clip the first long stitch at the notch on the right side of the inside of the sleeve. Draw up sleeve cap slightly to fit armhole, and fasten thread. Shrink out ease (p. 92, *BMCC*). With sleeve side up, stitch sleeve to armhole of dress. (See photos, page 63.) Sew one thread inside line of staystitching and ease line. Trim seam to ⅜ inch, and with sleeve side down, zigzag at machine. (See photo, page 70.) If you do not have a zigzag machine, make a second row of stitching ¼ inch from first row and pink near second stitching. Then, you may also wish to overcast by hand. However, a special attachment, called overcaster, is available for popular makes of straight-stitch machines.

With fabrics that are both sheer and crisp, such as organdy, the seams have a tendency to irritate a child's tender skin. To avoid this, spread the armhold seams and turn the edge of each seam toward the inside. Trim the seam allowance if it is too wide. Overcast the folded edges together. This makes a hand-turned French seam.

**Complete bodice unit.** Trim seam of cording to perfect ⅜ inch beyond stitching line to put in front waistline seam; this is the same width as first row of gathers from edge of skirt. Cording is used around entire waistline seam only when the dress does not have a sash. Before stitching on cording, at each side seam (A and A), pull out cord ⅝ inch and cut off. Then, restore shape of bias. Place raw edges of cording to meet raw edge of front of bodice. Using left side of zipper foot, stitch through same line of stitching on cording. Also, taper cording to nothing at side seams (A and A).

On outside of dress, stitch seam of sleeve and bodice ⅜ inch wide from sleeve down. Have armhole seam turned toward dress, because the corded edge of the facing may come too near the armhole and jam in machine. Press seam to one side or other so that well in seam will be eliminated when you turn to underside to complete stitching French seam. Trim seam to ⅛ inch, and to a point at edge of sleeve.

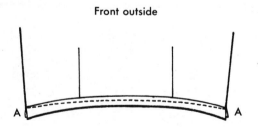

Front outside

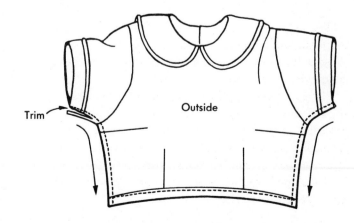

Trim

Outside

Stitch ¼-inch seam on underside from waist up; turn at edge of sleeve and stitch back for one inch.

The sleeves and bodice are always stitched in one operation on a child's dress, but never include any seams of any skirt at the same time.

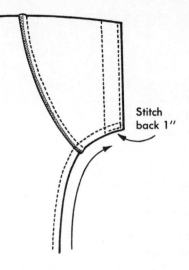

Stitch back 1″

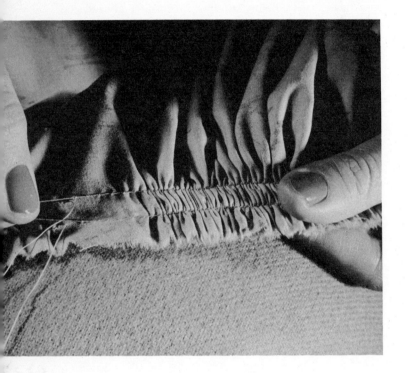

Pull up and tie gathering threads in each section of the skirt to fit bodice. Always pull the threads from the underside of the skirt and pull both of them in each section at one time. Do not make gathers on the placket opening at back.

With bodice side up, stitch bodice to skirt, using zipper foot; it is always needed when stitching cording. Turn right side of back facing to underside of skirt, and with bodice side up, sew facing through same line of stitching at waistline. Trim seam to ¼ inch, and round off to nothing at corners. Turn facings right side out, and beginning at end of facings, with gathers turned down, zigzag waistline seam at machine (see photograph, page 104). If you do not have a zigzag machine, make a second row of stitching ¼ inch from first row, and pink near second stitching. Then, you may also wish to overcast, by hand or by machine.

Using both hands and both wrists to hold gathers straight, and with a short stitch at machine, stitch through lower row of gathers for added strength.

We do not advise using elastic in the waistline seam of a child's dress.

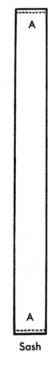

Sash

**Sash unit.** Sash is always torn lengthwise with one edge on selvage, if possible. Make a strip long enough for both pieces of sash, but do not cut in half until stitching is completed. Staystitch ends (A) ¼ inch from edge.

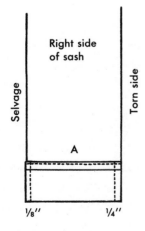

Turn and press raw edge on staystitching. Fold ends (A) to right side for 1¼ inches. On selvage side, stitch end ⅛ inch from edge, and on torn side ¼ inch from edge.

Turn right side out and press ends.  Stitch sash, turning back selvage ⅛ inch, and raw edge ⅛ inch each time for a double turn.

When stitching around ends, follow sketch, so that topstitching can be continuous.  Press sash.

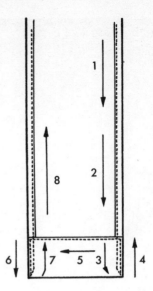

At half way mark, cut sash in two pieces.  At cut end make 3 pleats in sash; also, fold back hem ¼ or ⅜ inch.  Stitch ¼ inch from edge to hold in place.

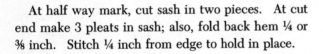

Sash

Place raw edge ¼ inch toward bodice back; stitch ¼ inch from edge in well of side seam, and make a second row on raw edge of sash.  Turn to back of dress and press in place.  If you would prefer a band in the front of the dress or belt in the back (or both), see second dress, pages 102–105.

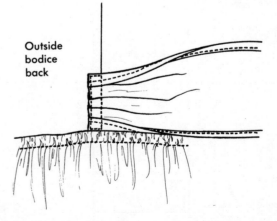

Outside
bodice
back

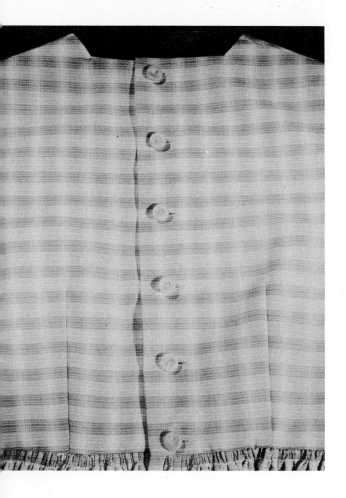

**Completed dress unit.** Make buttonholes in back of dress; the bottom buttonhole will be placed right at the top of the waistline seam. If the dress does not have a sash, use a hook and eye at the waistline, or a hook and a crocheted loop. Sew on buttons (page 84, *BMCC*).

We did not add any buttons for a trim below the collar on the front of the dress as commercially made ones so often have, because it is difficult to iron around them.

Final-press dress (Chapter 9, *BMCC*). For a French look on gathers, press flat for several inches below waistline.

### Basic learnings for a dress with bodice underlined

Underlining is desirable in the bodice of a child's dress for several reasons. It gives more support to the bodice for adding various trims, and for the weight of the full skirt. The bodice is more pleasing in appearance in sheer fabrics, and it is more durable. Lastly, underlining gives a quality look to a child's dress.

Fold

Sleeve

Front    Front band    Back

Back belt    Collar

Selvage    Tear three for skirt    Selvage

**Skirt unit.** Make precisely as in first dress, pages 84–87.

**Bodice back unit.** Cut bodice back and underlining ¼ inch wider than seamline for facing at edge A. In lighter weight fabrics, it is preferable to seam this edge rather than cut pieces double with a fold.

Staystitch neckline and shoulders just outside seamline in direction arrows indicate. Stitch darts; press to center back in bodice back, and to side edge in underlining.

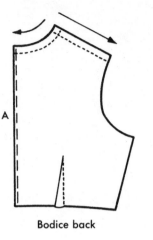
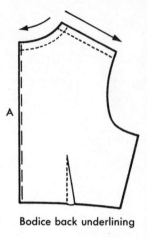

Bodice back                    Bodice back underlining

With right sides of back and back underlining placed together, stitch ¼-inch seam at A edge. Tear a lengthwise reinforcement strip for buttons and buttonholes, 1½ inches wide and length of bodice back. Place ¼ inch from seamline, and stitch ⅛ inch from edges B, C, and D, and ⅝ inch from lower edge E. Trim strip away ⅝ inch up to E. Understitch underlining at A edge, beginning one inch from top.

With right sides together, stitch neckline to center back on seamline. Clip to stitching at center back, and trim seam to ¼ inch, rounding off seam allowance in corner. Turn and press, and press understitched edge down the back.

Even if a child's dress had smocking in the front and could not be underlined for support, the back could still be done as you have just learned.

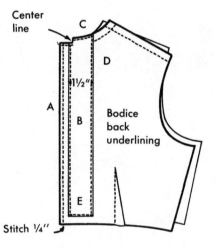

**Bodice front unit.** Staystitch neckline and shoulders just outside seamline and in direction arrows indicate on bodice front, and then on bodice front underlining. Stitch darts; press toward center front in bodice front, and toward side edge in underlining.

Bodice front

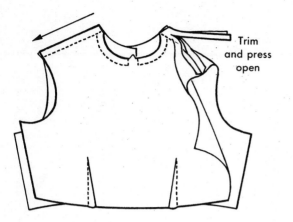

Trim
and press
open

**Bodice unit.** Stitch shoulder seams in direction arrows indicate on bodice and then on underlining. Trim to ⅜ inch and press open.

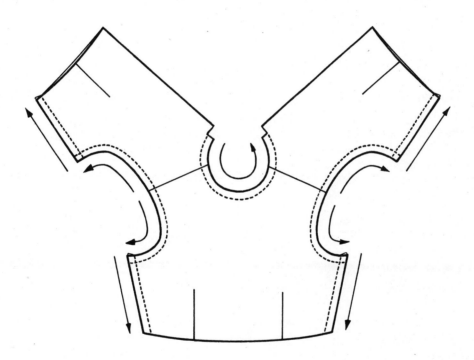

The inside of the bodice will face the inside of the underlining. Since the neckline has already been staystitched, you may disregard direction of grain, but staystitch neckline again *through both layers* just outside seamline from center back to center back.

Staystitch armholes and side edges together just outside seamline and in direction arrows indicate.

**Collar unit.** With shortest stitch machine will make, and with right sides together, stitch under collar to top collar along outer curved edge. Trim seam to a *very scant* ⅛ inch. Do not try to understitch this collar, because it is too small a circle.

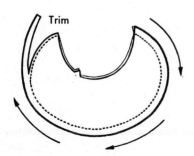

Trim

Turn right side out, and use a point former to round out edge of collar before pressing. Keep seam under point former when working around edge of collar; press collar.

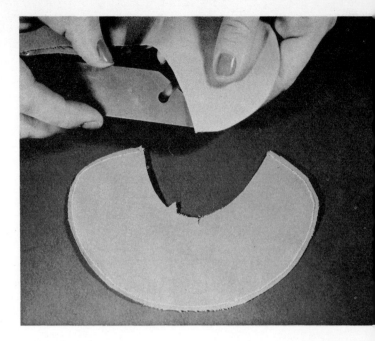

At neckline, stitch together top and under collar, just outside seamline. Key the two collars precisely and overstitch about 1 inch to hold together, so they will not slip or spread when attached to center front of bodice. If a trim is being used on collar that will extend to the neckline, put on trim at this time.

Place collar in position at center front and center back, and with dress side up, stitch collar to dress with ⅝-inch seam allowance (see sketch on page 90). Clip curve of dress and collar frequently up to seamline to straighten curve for ease in stitching. Trim entire neckline seam to scant ¼ inch.

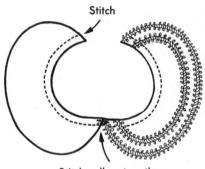

Stitch

Stitch collars together

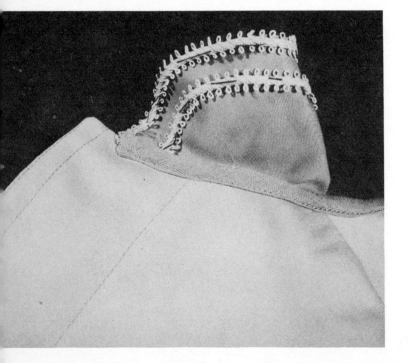

If the colors will match, you may use commercial cotton or rayon bias, or cut a piece one inch wide. With dress side up, sew on bias through previous stitching. Do not stretch bias; allow it to extend freely ¼ inch beyond center back. If necessary, trim width of bias, so it will just turn in a narrow amount and fit over scant ¼-inch seam. Commercial bias is usually trimmed to fold line of bias. Turn back raw edges at center back, and stitch bias flat to dress around neckline. We have eliminated facings at the neckline for ease in ironing.

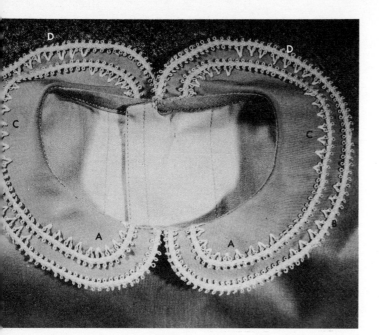

This is a photograph of the completed collar. The commercial trimming was tacked in place blindly. Then, an embroidery stitch with a contrasting color was used in a staggered fashion (A, B, C, and D) for a decorative effect. The same idea was repeated on the skirt.

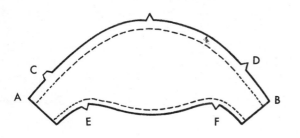

**Sleeve unit.** Staystitch cap of sleeve (A to B) exactly on seamline, changing to longer stitch at machine between notches (C to D). Staystitch lower edge of sleeve scant ⅜ inch from edge, changing to longer stitch at machine between notches (E to F).

To bind lower edge of sleeve, cut a bias strip 1½ inches wide and the length of a comfortable arm measurement for the child plus two seam allowances underarm. On the inside of the sleeve, clip the first long stitch at either E or F, and draw up sleeve to fit bias strip. With sleeve side up, stitch sleeve to bias, sewing one thread inside previous stitching. Trim seam to perfect ¼ inch. Turn over bias and press in place. Turn in raw edge of bias (A) and edge-stitch fold of it. The bias must be wide enough for the folded edge to extend about ⅛ inch beyond the stitching line on underside of the dress.

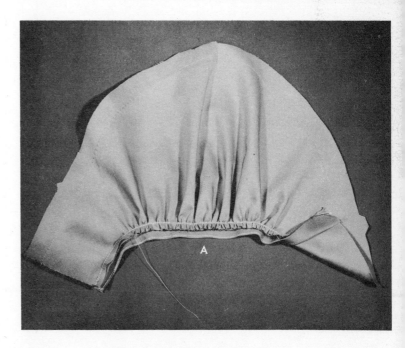

To prepare sleeve to be set in armhole, clip the first long stitch at the notch on the right side of the inside of the sleeve. Draw up sleeve to fit armhole and fasten thread. Distribute gathers, and with sleeve side up, stitch sleeve to armhole of dress. Sew one thread inside previous stitching (see photograph, page 63). Trim seam to ⅜ inch, and with gathers turned down, zigzag near edge of seam at machine (see photograph, page 70). If you do not have a zigzag machine, make a second row of stitching ¼ inch from first row, and pink near second edge. Then, you may also wish to overcast, either by hand or by machine.

With fabrics like organdy, finish the armhole seams as described on page 93 for the first dress.

**Back belt and front band unit.** The belt for the back of the dress is always torn lengthwise. Make a strip long enough for both parts of the belt, but do not cut in half until stitching is completed. If you would prefer a sash in the back or cording in the front of the dress (or both), see first dress (pages 93–97). Tear a lengthwise strip 3 inches wide and the width of lower edge of bodice back plus approximately 6 inches extra.

With right sides together, stitch ends and length of torn edges with ¼-inch seam; use shortest stitches at machine one inch each side of halfway mark (A). Trim corners, and at halfway mark, cut belt in two pieces. Press open seam on a dowel or ruler; turn belt right side out and press.

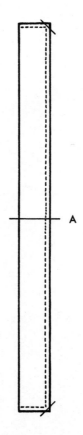

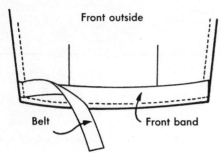

Front outside

Belt

Front band

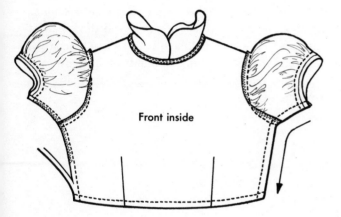

Front inside

The band for the front of the dress is always torn lengthwise. Tear it 3¼ inches wide (to finish 1¼ inches, same as belt, plus ⅜-inch seam allowance) and the width of lower edge of bodice front. With right sides out, fold in half and stitch raw edges together ⅜ inch from edge. Place raw edge of band to meet raw edge of bodice front, and stitch through previous stitching on band ⅜ inch from edge.

Place belts on sides of bodice front with folded edge at fold of band; lower edge of belts should key with ⅜-inch seamline. Stitch to dress just outside seamline.

**Complete bodice unit.** With right sides together, stitch seam of sleeve and bodice from sleeve down, including bias at lower edge of sleeve. The sleeves and bodice are always stitched in one operation on a child's dress, but never include any seams of any skirt at the same time.

Trim seam to ⅜ inch, and zigzag near edge of seam at machine.

Begin below bias on sleeve edge, and turn armhole seam toward sleeve. If you do not have a zigzag machine, make a second row of stitching ¼ inch from first row, and pink near second edge. Then, you may also wish to overcast.

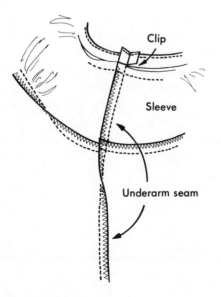

Clip

Sleeve

Underarm seam

Clip bias at end of zigzag stitch so it can lie open.

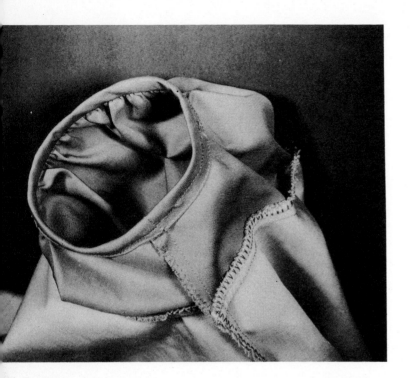

Restore turn of bias at seamline, and with sleeve side up, stitch bias in place through well at seamline.

Pull up and tie gathering threads in each section of the skirt to fit bodice. Always pull the threads from the underside of the skirt and pull both of them in each section at one time (see photograph, page 94). Do not make gathers on the placket opening at back.

With skirt side up, stitch bodice to skirt, sewing through first row of gathers ⅜ inch from seamline. With gathers turned down, zigzag waistline seam at machine. If you do not have a zigzag machine, make a second row of stitching ¼ inch from first row, and pink near second stitching. Then, you may also wish to overcast.

At back opening, turn in waistline seam at an angle (A), and bar tack at machine.

Using both hands and both wrists to hold gathers straight, and with a short stitch at the machine, stitch through lower row of gathers for added strength (see photograph, page 95).

We do not advise using elastic in the waistline seam of a child's dress.

**Completed dress unit.** Make buttonholes in the back of the dress and in the belt. The bottom buttonhole on the dress will be placed right at the top of the waistline seam (see photograph, page 97). If the dress does not have a belt, use a hook and eye at the waistline, or a hook and a crocheted loop. Sew buttons on dress and belt (pages 84–85, *BMCC*).

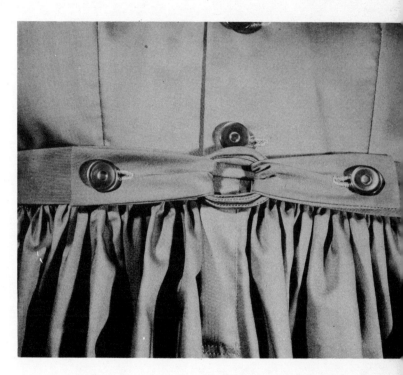

The belt may overlap about 3 inches and be fastened with two buttons and buttonholes.

The ends of the one in the photograph go through a triple ring of bias tubing and fasten back on the belt with buttons and buttonholes.

If trim is used on skirt, a seam may be opened to insert raw edge of trim; stitch seam again. However, trim may be applied before skirt is put together at last seam.

Final-press dress (Chapter 9, *BMCC*). For a French look on gathers, press flat for several inches below waistline.

**Additional suggestions for quality looking dresses.**

Every little girl should have a fine broadcloth smocked dress. The hem of this dress features the technique for lengthening shown on page 109. The embroidery is done on the top of the hem, and then the hem is sewn by hand to the dress.

The top of this organdy pinafore is underlined as shown on pages 97–99. The hem features the technique for lengthening shown on page 109. The trimming is sewn fast to the top of the hem, and then the hem is sewn by hand to the dress.

The facings for this dress are cut like those for the blouse on page 35, *BMCC*. This simplifies finishing the neckline and reinforcing the armholes.

Sew together shoulder seams of front and back bodice. Then, stitch bias cording to neckline of bodice just as you learned to do on the top collar, page 89.

Sew shoulder seams of facings, and apply facings to bodice just as you learned to do on under collar, page 90.

Staystitch armhole edges together, and proceed with techniques for completing dress that you have learned in this chapter.

## Children's dresses

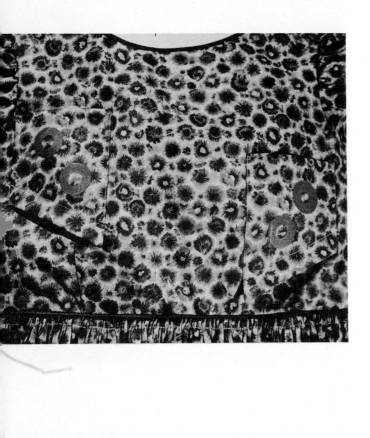

The pockets on this dress are trimmed with Bondex, which comes in assorted colors and can be cut into desirable shapes and ironed on garments.

The bias on the sleeves, bodice, waistline, and skirt of this dress were done as in the photograph shown on page 225.

The two parts of the sash were made on the bias, and the bias band at the front was topstitched over them (A and A).

By clipping seam (A) and turning it to right side of dress under hem, the hem can be lowered on right side of dress (B), and creases or the worn hem edge will not show.

This is not possible on ready-to-wear, but you can stitch a narrow tuck at crease or worn hem edge before hemming dress. Another possibility is to add a trim such as braid over the crease or worn hem edge.

# Chapter 9

# Short shorts, pedal pushers, bermuda shorts, and slacks for women and girls

Most likely, there will not be another chapter in this book that will mean more to the American girl and woman than this one. It isn't that they cannot buy short shorts, pedal pushers, bermuda shorts, and slacks, but that they cannot buy them to fit, or even have them altered to fit. We find more ill-fitting pants on the American woman than good-fitting ones. *A good fit starts in the cutting for the individual figure.*

Many of the techniques in fitting and cutting-to-fit will be similar to those for a skirt on pages 65–70, *Bishop Method of Clothing Construction.*[*] Also, you will need to use the skirt key grain lines on page 49, *BMCC.* Work with an inexpensive piece of fabric to perfect the fit of pants for your individual figure; then, you can apply your learnings to any of them you make in the future.

Whether you are tall or short, take the hip measurement over the largest part of the hips to determine pattern size. It is important for slacks to fit as closely as possible at the hip because of the shaping of the crotch. Proportioned slacks fit as far as height is concerned.

The following cutting-to-fit suggestions are the most common ones needed for the majority of women on any length of pants.

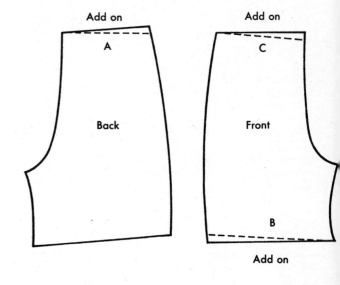

### Cutting-to-fit

At A, ½ inch to as much as one inch can be added at the side back for the figure that has fullness at the side hipline, and side seams swing toward front.

At B, add a corresponding amount, so that side seams will match with perfection. Do not add as much as you did at the back, however, if B edge will fall below straight of grain at side edge. In that case, ease difference on back to front of shorts.

At C, approximately ½ inch can be added (not more than will make it straight of grain at center front) for the person who has fullness in the front of her figure.

---

[*] Hereafter referred to as *BMCC.*

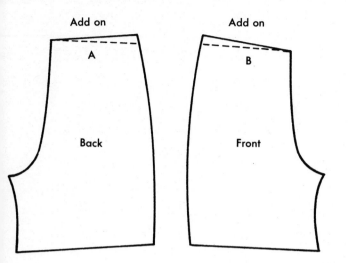

If the figure has fullness at side hipline on both the front and back (see former sketch for back only), ½ inch to as much as one inch can be added on waist edge at side seam (A and B), tapering to nothing at center front and center back. If the grain tells you to do so, you may add a little extra at the center front, also.

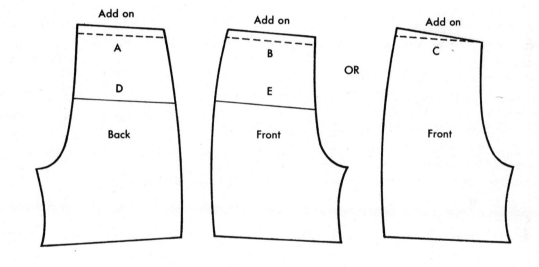

OR

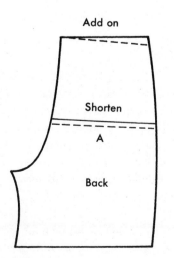

If the figure is full across the back of the hips, or if the figure requires a longer crotch, add needed amount of fabric on waist edge of pants back (A). On the front, needed amount of fabric may either be added all the way across waist edge (B) or tapered from side seam to nothing at center front (C). It may be added at D and E (line indicated on pattern) instead of A and B, if the figure is wide in the hip.

If the figure is flat in the hips, take out necessary amount by making an even fold (A) in pattern halfway down crotch seam. Then, add a corresponding amount at waist edge tapering to nothing at center back, so that side seams will match with perfection. See sketch on page 112 also.

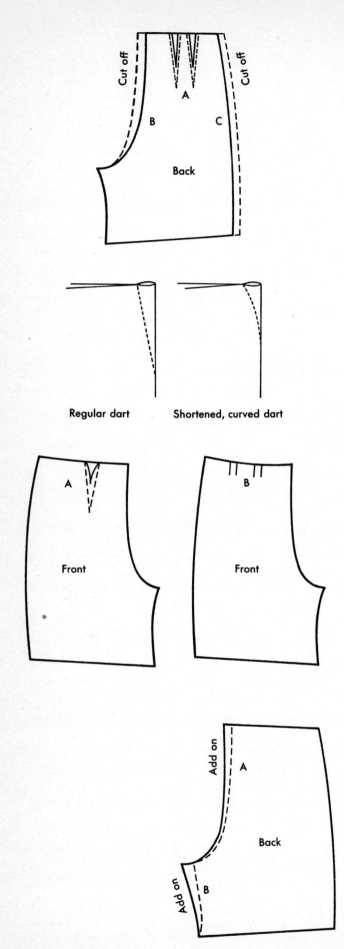

Very often, there is too much pick-up in the darts for the fullness in the figure. Then, make two small darts (A), or one dart instead of two, and the excess fullness in the back of the pants can either be cut out at B, or cut off all the way down at C. When you cut off the fabric at B, the pants will fit better for a heavier leg.

Frequently, on the front of the pants, the long, straight dart stitches out fabric that is needed for ease in the fit of the figure. Then, the shortened, curved dart (A) is preferred, because it will give more fabric where it is needed, or one or two tucks (B) may be folded where ease is needed, instead of using the dart.

When cutting pants from plaid or striped fabric, the design will be improved on the back if line is made straighter than pattern at A. Add corresponding amount at B to front and back. If the figure is heavy in the thighs, add fabric all the way down at B as shown in the second sketch. This alteration will also improve the fit of pants for figures that are flat in the back (see sketch on page 111).

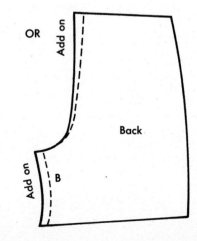

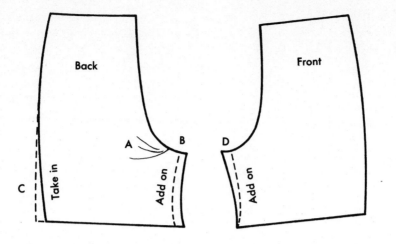

When pants sink in at crotch (A), and pull or wrinkle at the same place across the front, it is because they need more room on the inside of the leg (B).

If the pants look wide across the back when necessary amount has been added at B, taper side seams (C).

Add corresponding amount at D, tapering to nothing at lower edge.

It may be necessary to add all the way down the front at D. If so, the side seams of the front may be tapered, also.

This is a valued alteration for the person who has a heavy inside leg.

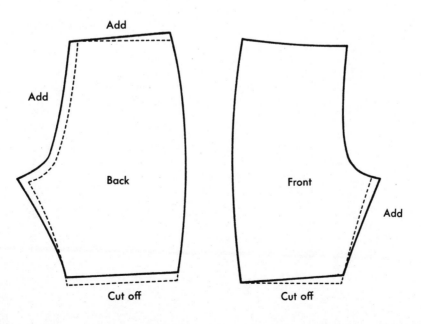

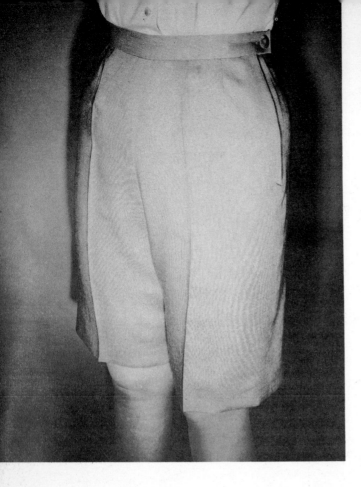
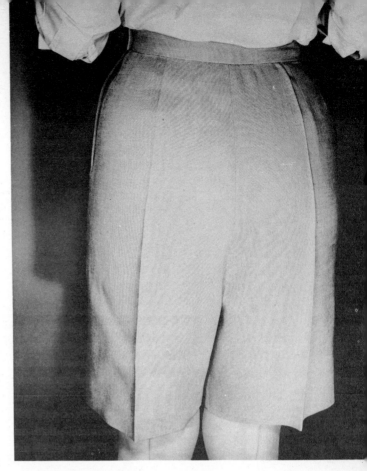

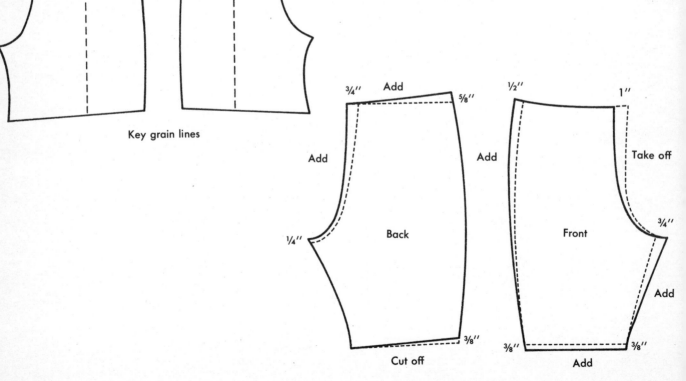

The bermuda shorts in the photographs have been fitted to grain perfection, using the two all-important key grain lines on the sketch.

These alterations were made on a size 14 pattern to the bermuda shorts in the above photographs.

Key grain lines

Back

Front

¾″    Add    ⅝″

Add              Add

¼″

                          ½″              1″

                          Take off

                                         ¾″

                                         Add

⅜″

Cut off

⅜″    Add    ⅜″

## Short shorts

The short shorts may be underlined, if desired, with the same techniques shown with bermuda shorts, pages 128–133. If they are not underlined, make as follows:

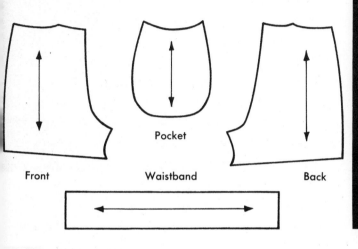

Front        Waistband        Back

Pocket

**Back unit.** Staystitch waist edge and right back of shorts from notch up just outside seamline and in the direction shown with arrows on sketch.

Staystitch left back of shorts from notch up and lower edges scant ¼ inch from edge and in the direction shown with arrows on sketch.

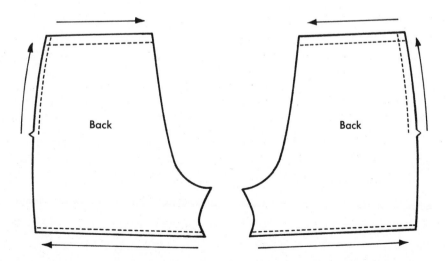

Back        Back

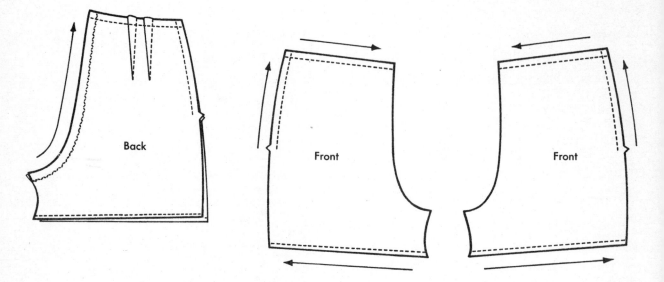

Sew seam at crotch in direction shown. Considerable strain is placed on this seam; strengthen it by stitching with machine set one point or even less to zigzag. If you do not have a zigzag machine, sew with shortest stitch at machine.

Set the machine more than one point to zigzag and stitch both sides of seam ¼ inch from edge. Stretch seam in curve only. If you do not have a zigzag machine, staystitch seam, and stretch in curved area, also. Press open seam.

Stitch darts (page 27, *BMCC*) and press toward center back.

**Front unit.** Staystitch waist edge and sides of shorts from notch up just outside the seamline and in direction shown with arrows on sketch. Staystitch lower edges scant ¼ inch from edge and in the direction shown with arrows on the sketch.

Sew seam at crotch in direction shown. Considerable strain is placed on this seam; strengthen it by stitching with machine set one point or even less to zigzag. If you do not have a zigzag machine, sew with shortest stitch at machine.

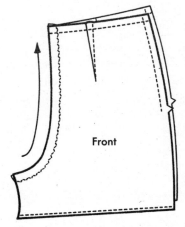

Set the machine more than one point to zigzag and stitch both sides of seam ¼ inch from edge. Stretch seam in curve only. If you do not have a zigzag machine, staystitch seam and stretch in curved area, also. Press open seam.

Stitch darts (page 27, *BMCC*) and press toward center front.

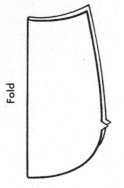

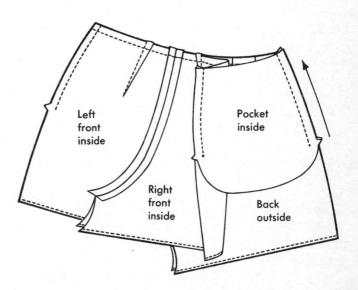

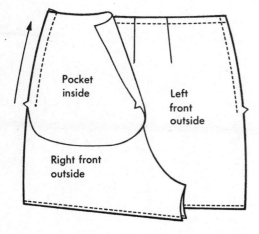

**Pocket unit.** Cut pocket on the fold for a smooth line in shorts. Use one pocket on the right front of shorts.

With right sides together, stitch front pocket piece to front of shorts from notch to the waist edge. Lockstitch securely and precisely at notch or other pattern marking for pocket opening.

With right sides together, stitch back pocket piece to back of shorts from notch to the waist edge. Lockstitch securely and precisely at notch or other pattern marking for pocket opening.

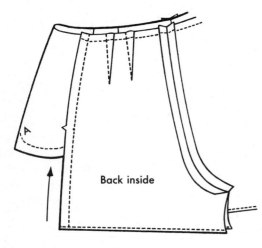

Back inside

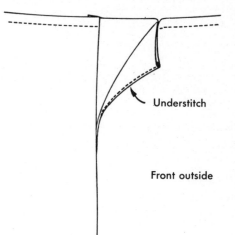

Understitch

Front outside

Join front and back unit of shorts by stitching side seam from lower edge up to pocket opening; this connects the stitching line of the pocket pieces.

Check the cut of shorts for direction to sew side seams. If the style is tapered at lower edge, always key lockstitching on pocket pieces and sew from lockstitching down to lower edge.

Then, place the shorts away from the pocket pieces, and starting exactly at lockstitching, close pocket pieces from notch to fold of pocket, rounding off stitching in corner to keep lint out (A).

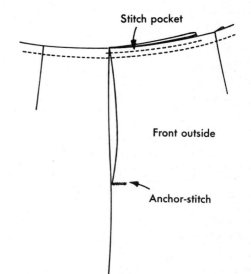

Stitch pocket

Front outside

Anchor-stitch

Trim the front side seam to ¼ inch, and understitch edge of front pocket piece length of pocket opening.

Place pocket in position on front of shorts, matching upper edges with waist edge. Stitch in place.

Press the back side seam toward back of shorts, and below the pocket opening; front pocket seam is pressed toward the front. Anchor-stitch at lower edge of opening.

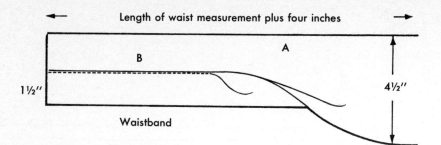

Length of waist measurement plus four inches

B           A

1½″                               4½″

Waistband

**Zipper unit.** On left side of shorts, stitch side seam and insert placket zipper precisely like series of learnings on pp. 40–41, *BMCC.*

**Waistband unit.** The waistband, to finish 1¼ inches wide, is made from a lengthwise torn strip 4½ inches wide and about 4 inches longer than individual waist measurement. With a crosswise-ribbed fabric such as bengaline, a crosswise strip would be used for the band.

With automatic hem gauge, make a lengthwise fold to the inside 1½ inches deep, and press. Stitch close to raw edge (B) of folded section; this forms the band's own interfacing.

To attach the waistband to the shorts, place the right side of band (edge A) to the wrong side of shorts. Pin first at center front (R), allowing enough additional band to extend to front placket opening plus 1¼ inches extra (S).

Measure one-half of waist measurement and allow that much band to center back of shorts (T). Pin in place. The size is accurate from center front to center back. For example, if the waist measures 28 inches, the amount of band from center front to center back would be 14 inches.

Next, fold the shorts from center front to center back to measure one-half of them, and mark with a pin (U). Repeat with the band (U) and bring together the two pins. The pattern manufacturer has given tolerance on shorts to allow them to fall softly over normal body curves, and this will aid in distributing it evenly; pin shorts to band at intervals. The halfway mark on the shorts (U) will not be the side seam, because the front of the shorts is always cut wider than the back of the shorts.

To measure the amount of band needed for the second half of the back of the shorts, fold loose end of the band carefully back to the side seam. Mark with a pin on the band the exact seamline. Place the pin on seamline of zipper edge of other half of back of shorts (V). Distribute ease evenly and pin band to shorts at intervals. Repeat for second half of band front and front of shorts, and pin at S.

Sew band to shorts on seamline with band side up. It is easier to control the ease on shorts when it is on the underside, and you will be able to follow a check, stripe, or ridge on band (when fabric has such a design) for perfection in stitching and in appearance on outside of band.

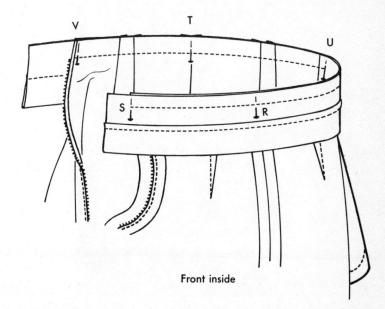

Front inside

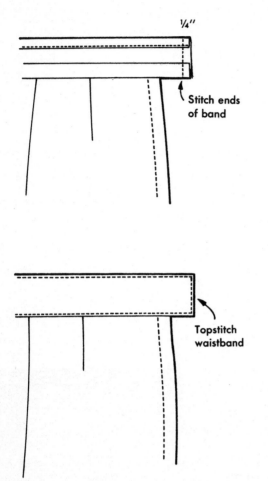

¼"

Stitch ends
of band

Topstitch
waistband

Press seam up. To stitch ends of band, fold right sides together and stitch ¼-inch seam. The belt extends one inch on the front and laps under approximately two inches on the back.

Trim seam to ¼ inch and round off seam allowance at top corners. Turn band to outside of shorts and pin in place.

The band is already turned in with perfection and is ready to topstitch on lower edge over seamline on shorts. Continue to topstitch all around band.

Finish ends of band with two buttons and two machine buttonholes. To sew on buttons, see pp. 84 and 85, *BMCC*.

**Hem unit.** Using automatic hem gauge, turn under raw edge ¼ inch and press. Then, turn up hem 1¼ inches and press. Repeat for second half of shorts.

Stitch inside leg seams from the top down and press open.

Hem shorts at machine as in bottom photograph, page 46, *BMCC.*

Final-press shorts (Chapter 9, *BMCC*).

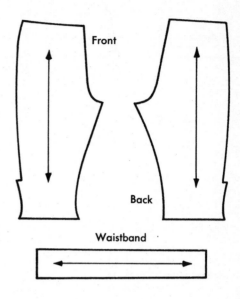

## Pedal pushers

The pedal pushers may be underlined, if desired, with the same techniques shown with bermuda shorts, pages 128–133. If they are not underlined, make as follows:

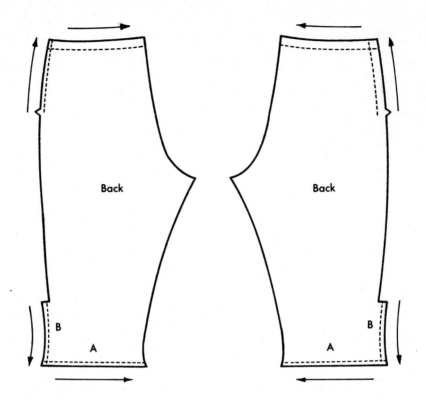

**Back unit.** Staystitch waist edge and right back of pedal pushers from notch up just outside seamline, and in the direction shown with arrows on sketch.

Staystitch left back of pedal pushers from notch up and edges A and B scant ¼ inch from edge and in the direction shown with arrows on sketch. If pattern for pedal pushers has a fitted facing at lower edge, see techniques at end of this section.

Sew seam at crotch in direction shown. Considerable strain is placed on this seam; strengthen it by stitching with machine set one point or even less to zigzag. If you do not have a zigzag machine, sew with shortest stitch at machine.

Set the machine more than one point to zigzag and stitch both sides of seam ¼ inch from edge. Stretch seam in curve only. If you do not have a zigzag machine, staystitch seam and stretch in curved area, also. Press open seam.

Stitch darts (page 27, *BMCC*) and press toward center back.

Using automatic hem gauge, turn under raw edge at A ¼ inch and press. Then, turn up hem 1¼ inches and press (C).

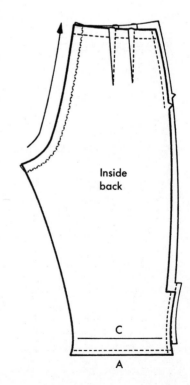

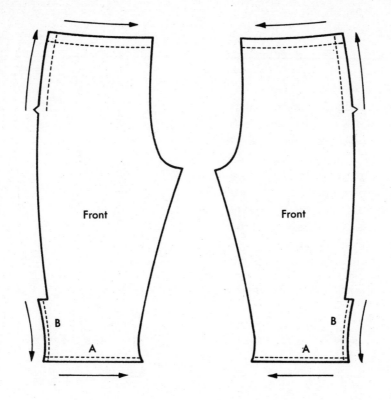

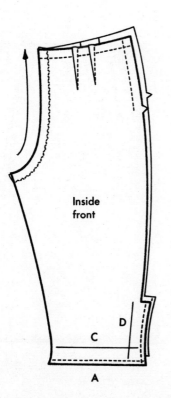

**Front unit.** Staystitch waist edge and sides of pedal pushers from notch up just outside the seamline and in direction shown with arrows on sketch.

Staystitch edges A and B scant ¼ inch from edge and in the direction shown with arrows on sketch.

Sew seam at crotch in direction shown. Considerable strain is placed on this seam; strengthen it by stitching with machine set one point or even less to zigzag. If you do not have a zigzag machine, sew with shortest stitch at machine.

Set the machine more than one point to zigzag and stitch both sides of seam ¼ inch from edge. Stretch seam in curve only. If you do not have a zigzag machine, staystitch seam and stretch in curved area, also. Press open seam.

Stitch darts (page 27, *BMCC*) and press toward center front.

Using automatic hem gauge, turn under raw edge at A ¼ inch and press. Then, turn up hem 1¼ inches and press (C). Turn extension to inside on pattern fold line (D) and press.

**Complete unit.** If a pocket is desired on the right side of pedal pushers, follow the techniques for pocket in short shorts described on pages 117–118.

Sew side seams from waist edge to pattern marking for opening (A). Edges are staystitched above notches, thus making it possible to stitch off grain in this short area. Leave left side open above notch for placket zipper. On back of pedal pushers, clip to stitching at pattern marking for opening (A). Next, sew inside leg seams from top down. Pink seams with pinking shears, if necessary, and press open. Restore hem line at lower edges in pressing.

Hem pedal pushers at machine as in bottom photograph, page 46, *BMCC*.

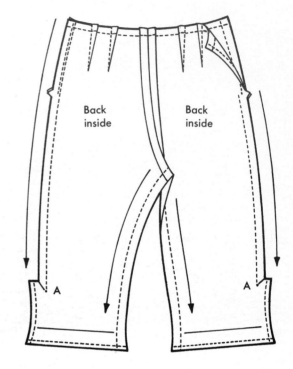

**Zipper unit.** On left side of pedal pushers, insert placket zipper precisely like series of learnings on pages 40–41, *BMCC*.

**Side openings at lower edge.** *1. Back.* Turn in raw edge on ¼-inch staystitching and turn again to make ½ inch wide hem. Press. Stitch near edge of hem (A) at machine, and form a triangle (B) at lower edge as shown.

*2. Front.* The front of the opening is already pressed on pattern marking line (C). Turn in raw edge on ¼-inch staystitching and stitch across bottom (D), up the hem near folded edge (E), and back and forth through front and back (F) for reinforcement.

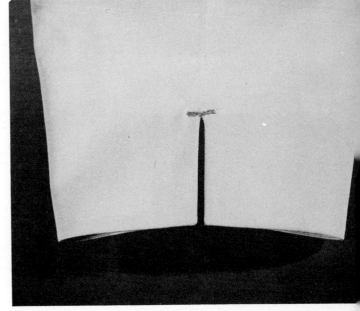

This photograph shows the completed opening from the topside.

**Waistband unit.**  The waistband is put on precisely like the series of learnings on pages 119–120 for short shorts.

Final-press pedal pushers (Chapter 9, *BMCC*).

**Fitted facing at lower edge.**  If the pattern has a fitted facing at lower edge of pedal pushers, staystitch lower edges of pedal pushers (A), front and back, and facings (B) just outside seamline.  Staystitch top of facings (C), front and back, scant ¼ inch from edge.

Clean-finish upper edges of facings (C).  To clean-finish, turn under on ¼-inch staystitching line and stitch close to folded edge.

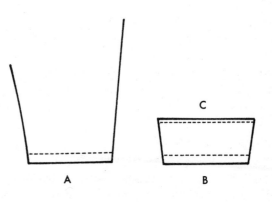

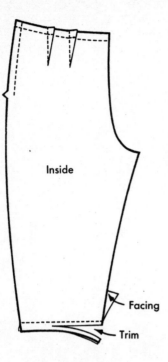

Right sides together and pedal pushers turned up, sew facings to lower edges, front and back. Trim seam to scant ¼ inch, and understitch edge, beginning and ending one inch from edges. Understitching is a row of machine stitching along the edge of the facing that catches the two trimmed seams to the facing.

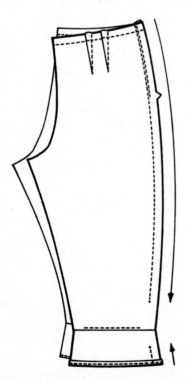

Sew side seams of pedal pushers from waist edge to pattern marking for opening. Edges are staystitched above notches, thus making it possible to stitch off grain in this short area. Leave left side open above notch for placket zipper. Sew side seams of facing down to pattern marking for opening.

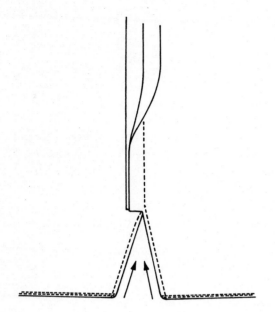

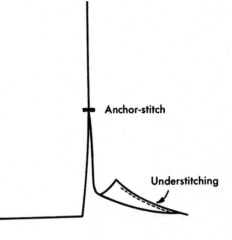

Anchor-stitch edge of opening.

Right sides together, and beginning at lower edge of pedal pushers, close point of opening down to pattern marking for opening. Repeat for second half of point. Round off seam allowance in corners and trim seams to ¼ inch. Trim remainder of facing seam to ¼ inch.

Turn right side out and press. Press open side seam and facing seam.

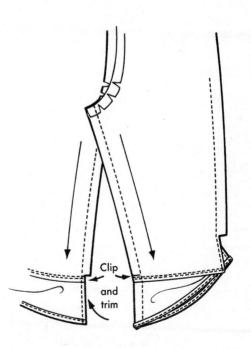

Open out facing at inside leg seam and sew inside leg seam and facing from crotch down. Press open seam. Clip up to stitching at seamline at fold of facing, and trim facing seam to ¼ inch. Turn back facing and press.

Stitch hem at machine same as other pedal pushers and short shorts.

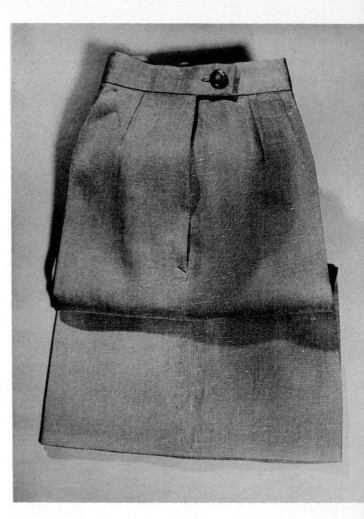

### Lined bermuda shorts

All of the quality-looking bermuda shorts are under-lined. However, they can be made without under-lining, following the techniques for short shorts at the beginning of this chapter, just as short shorts, pedal pushers, and slacks could be underlined, using the techniques from this section.

Popular underlinings are cotton broadcloth, cotton percale, rayon twill, and super soft siri.

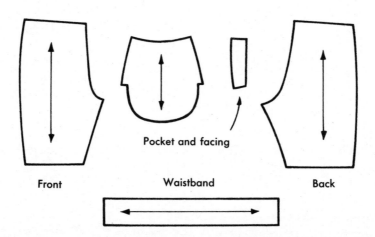

Front          Pocket and facing          Back

Waistband

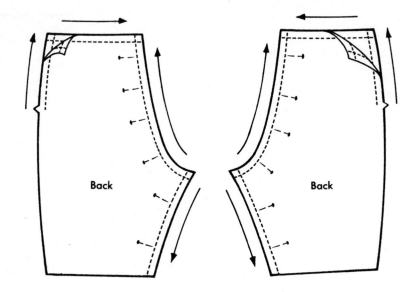

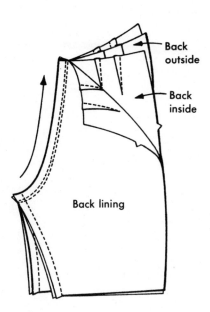

**Back unit.** Place underlining fabric to inside of shorts fabric. Pin together at crotch seam and inside leg seam. *Separately*, staystitch shorts and underlining at waist edge and sides from notch up, just outside the seamline, and in direction shown with arrows on sketch.

*Together*, staystitch crotch seam and inside leg seam just outside seamline, and in direction shown. On one half, the underlining will be on top; on other half, shorts will be on top. With loosely woven fabric for shorts, it may be difficult to sew with shorts on top and underlining below. Then, guard grain very cautiously and sew against it—with underlining on top.

Sew seam at crotch in direction shown. Considerable strain is placed on this seam; strengthen it by stitching with machine set one point or even less to zigzag. If you do not have a zigzag machine, sew with shortest stitch at machine.

Set the machine more than one point to zigzag and stitch both sides of seam ¼ inch from edge. Stretch seam in curve only. If you do not have a zigzag machine, staystitch seam and stretch in curved area, also. Press open seam.

Separately, stitch darts (page 27, *BMCC*), so that underside of darts in shorts and in underlining will face each other. Press darts in shorts to center front and in underlining to side edge.

Sometimes, the darts are not stitched in underlining and are just folded in place.

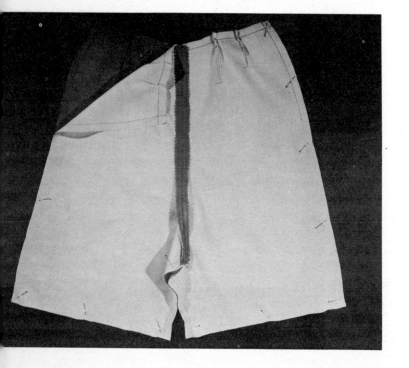

**Front Unit.** The front unit is made following the techniques above for the back unit.

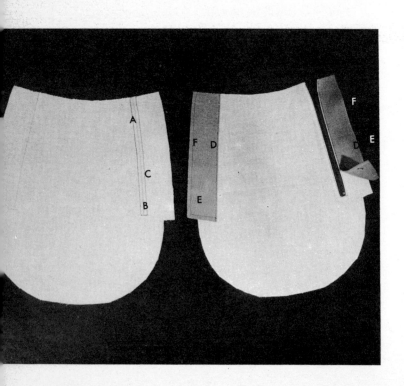

**Pocket unit.** On pattern marking line (A) for zipper insertion in left pocket, staystitch for length of zipper and tape at top. Cross over at lower edge of staystitching (B) and make a second row of stitching (C) ⅜ inch from first row. Slash between rows of staystitching and into corners at lower edge. Press under raw edges on staystitching. With zipper foot, stitch pocket piece close to metal of zipper.

Staystitch D edges of pocket facings scant ¼ inch from edge. Press under raw edge on staystitching. With the zipper foot, stitch D edge of pocket facing close to metal of zipper. With regular presser foot, stitch D edge in place on other half of pocket, and stitch E and F raw edges to pocket, ¼ inch from edge.

Make a second pocket for right side, if desired.

Insert the pocket with the same series of steps shown with short shorts on pages 117–118.

On front and back pocket seam, trim muslin to seamline. Stagger remaining edges of front seam in trimming, making upper one ¼ inch and under one ⅛ inch. Understitch edge of front pocket (A) length of pocket opening. Open the zipper, and place remainder of pocket in place on front of shorts, matching upper edges with waist edge (B). Stitch in place.

Press open the side seam below the zipper. Anchor-stitch at lower edges of pocket opening. If right pocket is used, anchor-stitch one inch down from upper edge, also.

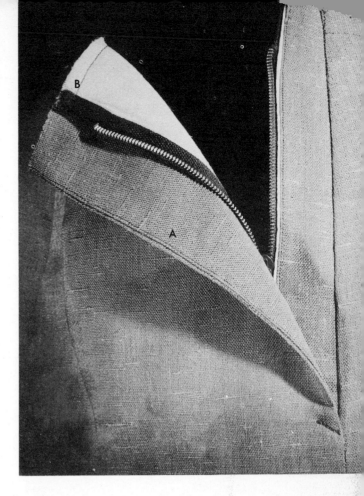

**Underlining unit.** Going from top down, stitch side seams of underlining so that raw edges of seams will face shorts. Press open seams.

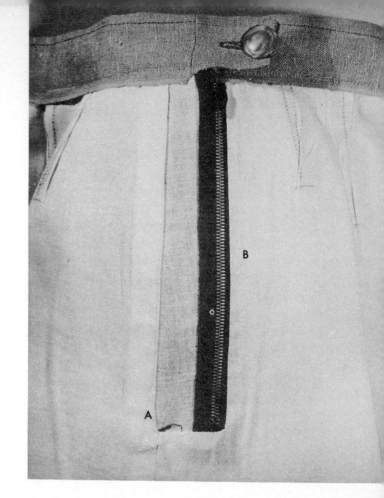

On left side, leave open seam to bottom of metal part of zipper. At A, clip to lockstitching on back seam allowance; lay raw edge of underlining to meet raw edge of shorts' side seam. Zigzag raw edges together at machine, or slipstitch by hand.

Keep zipper closed. Lay underlining in place on front of shorts. Chalk mark or pin mark where you can feel the front edge of metal zipper on underlining (B). Staystitch this mark, and also straight across lower edge of metal zipper to lockstitching on side seam of underlining. Beginning above lockstitching, cut underlining at an angle into staystitching at corner. Trim away excess fabric, leaving ½-inch seam allowance to turn under to staystitching. Whipstitch underlining in place along stitching line on front placket edge, and on lower edge over to lockstitching at seamline.

With underlining on top, stitch together raw edges of shorts and underlining at the waistline, just outside the seamline.

**Waistband unit.** If bermuda shorts are being made of a lightweight fabric such as cotton cord, waistband will be made and put on precisely like the short shorts pages 119–120). However, if shorts are being made of linen, lightweight wool, etc., use the following technique.

The waistband (to finish 1¼ inches wide) is made from a lengthwise-torn strip 3½ inches wide and about 4 inches longer than the individual waist measurement. Tear with one edge along the selvage. With a crosswise-ribbed fabric such as bengaline, it is a crosswise strip for the band.

Interfacing (underlining fabric is usually satisfactory) is also a lengthwise-torn strip 2 inches wide.

Place interfacing ¼ inch from torn edge of band and stitch in place near edge of interfacing. Then, stitch second edge of interfacing to band. It is not necessary to press band before stitching second edge, as we learned to do on page 170, *BMCC*, for heavier fabrics in tailoring a suit. Try band around waistline, and hold with firmness one likes in fit of band, to determine size needed.

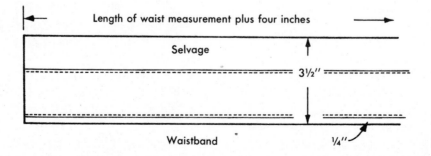

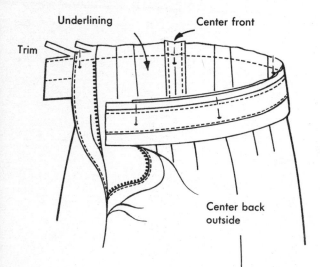

Underlining    Center front

Trim

Center back
outside

Selvage will fall in place ⅜ inch below seamline on back of shorts; pin to hold in place. (See photo page 132.) With shorts right side up, stitch in well on seamline to hold band in place.

Final-press the band. Finish ends with two large metal hooks and eyes, a double set of large snaps, or two buttons and buttonholes.

To attach waistband to shorts, open zipper and place torn edge of band to meet waist edge of shorts, right sides together. Pin first at center front, allowing enough additional band to extend to edge of left front pocket opening, plus a seam allowance extra.

Proceed with pinning on band exactly as you learned to do with the skirt on page 43, *BMCC*, or short shorts, pages 119–120.

Sew band to shorts on seamline with band side up. It is easier to control the ease on shorts when it is on the underside, and you will be able to follow a check, stripe, or ridge on band (when fabric has such a design) for perfection in stitching and in appearance on outside of band. Press seam up and trim band seam allowance to ¼ inch and shorts to ⅜ inch.

To finish ends of band, fold right sides together. Bring selvage edge ⅜ inch over seamline on front of band. On back of band, stitch band parallel to edge of pocket opening, and on front of band to extend 1½ inches. Trim seams on both ends to ¼ inch and round off corners. Turn ends right side out and press.

**Hem unit.** Trim seam in hem of shorts to ¼ inch, going a little beyond fold of hem. With underlining side up, stitch underlining and shorts together 1¼ inches from raw edge (A). Using hem gauge, turn up 1½ inches and press lower edge of shorts and underlining together. Previous stitching will be ¼ inch from fold of hem; trim away underlining to stitching.

Staystitch or zigzag shorts ¼ inch from raw edge of hem (B). Pink with pinking shears, if necessary.

Stitch inside leg seams from top down, and press open. Trim seam in hem of shorts to ¼ inch, going a little beyond fold of hem.

Stitch hem to underlining by hand, using pick stitch on underside of hem (page 82, *BMCC*).

Final-press shorts, Chapter 9, *BMCC*.

## Slacks

We are not showing the techniques from beginning to end for making the slacks, because the side pockets and the zipper are exactly like the bermuda shorts on pages 128–133.

Then, everything else, including the waistband, is done like men's slacks in Chapter 12. The band will vary only in that it finishes at the side instead of center front of slacks. The back pocket is usually eliminated in women's slacks.

These women's slacks were not cuffed, because they are too tapered.

On both men's and women's slacks, use metal hooks and eyes or large snaps.

Chapter **10**

# Shirts for men, women, and children

Try these techniques on one shirt, and you will have learned them for every shirt. Each one you make will be easier and will go faster. Cut out several and complete the same unit on each one to save time. Cut out a dozen to make for Christmas gifts. A shirt you have made personally will delight young and old alike, and will truly be his or her favorite.

The yoke of the shirt is cut lengthwise. The cuffs and collar are cut lengthwise and on a fold. Firm (drip-dry) siri has been used in the collar, cuffs, and front of the shirt in the photographs. The shirt was made of a medium-weight, textured cotton fabric. In a lighter weight fabric, use a lighter weight interfacing. Shrink siri for garments that will be laundered in hot water.

Buy a man's shirt pattern according to chest measurement. If the man's neck is much larger than the pattern size, increase neck size by cutting neckline larger at the shoulders, and increase collar size.

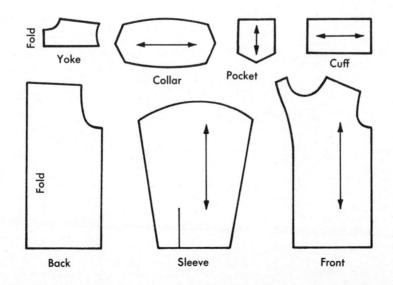

Fold — Yoke — Collar — Pocket — Cuff — Fold — Back — Sleeve — Front

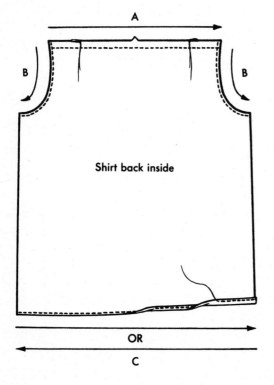

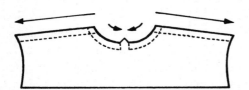

## Shirt back unit

The pleats give a better line to the shirt back, when they are placed near the armhole edge.

Fold pleats toward armholes at top of shirt back (A). They are held in place with staystitching, placed just outside the seamline. Staystitch armholes (B) and bottom of shirt (C) ⅛ inch from edge in direction shown. To hem shirt back, turn in raw edge on stay-stitching line, fold up narrow hem, and stitch at machine along upper edge.

If you make a heavier wool shirt, it is desirable to cut the yoke facing from a rayon twill fabric. The yoke and yoke facing are always cut lengthwise. Staystitch each of them separately at the neckline and shoulders just outside seamline in direction shown.

With right sides together, *and with shirt side up,* sew yoke to shirt back.

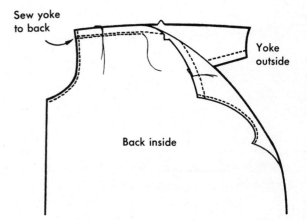

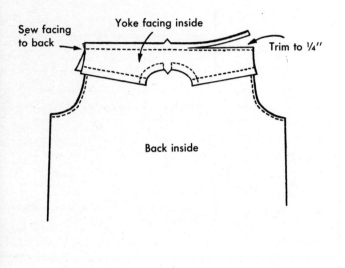

Sew facing to back

Yoke facing inside

Trim to ¼″

Back inside

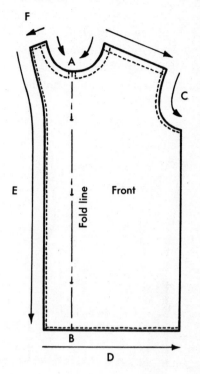

F

A

C

E

Fold line

Front

B

D

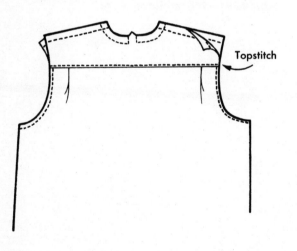

Topstitch

With right side of yoke facing to inside of shirt back, but with yoke side up, sew facing to shirt back through the row of stitching on the seamline.

Press up yoke and facing and trim seam to ¼ inch.

Topstitch on yoke, close to seam, through all thicknesses. In plain fabric, make a second row of topstitching ¼ inch from first row.

## Shirt front unit

Clip fold line for facing on shirt front for ⅛ inch at A and B. To press, fold back facing in place; on underside, mark one layer of fabric only with tracing paper and wheel. Through both layers of fabric, place 3 or 4 pins in marking line. Turn back and press top layer on pin line (see photographs, page 164). Remove pins. Turn fabric to have under layer on top. Fold back top layer to meet under fold and press second side. Staystitch neckline and shoulders just outside seamline in direction shown. Staystitch armholes (C), bottom of shirt (D), and edges of facing (E and F) ⅛ inch from edge, and in direction shown. Clean-finish edges E and F of facing. To clean-finish, turn under on staystitching line and stitch close to folded edge (page 74, *The Bishop Method of Clothing Construction*°).

°Hereafter referred to as *BMCC*.

Tear a lengthwise strip of interfacing (1½ to 2 inches wide) to reinforce shirt front for buttons and buttonholes. It will extend to the top of the shirt and one inch below lower button and buttonhole. Place ⅛-inch from fold line. Stitch in place at edges C and D. At edges A and B, stitching will extend only to top button and buttonhole (E). If edge B is cut on the selvage, it does not require stitching to facing.

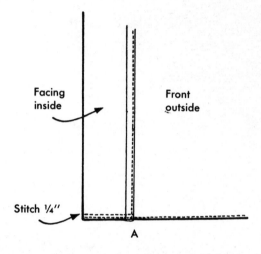

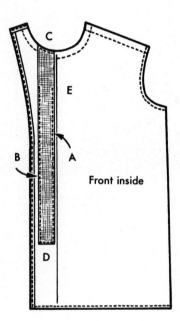

At lower edge, turn facing to outside on fold line. With right sides together, stitch a ¼-inch seam to edge of facing. Trim away corner, turn, and press. On shirt front, at edge of facing (A), clip to stay-stitching ⅛ inch from lower edge.

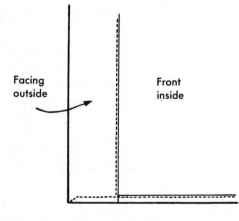

Stitch hem same as shirt back, and continue to top-stitch lower edge of facing as shown.

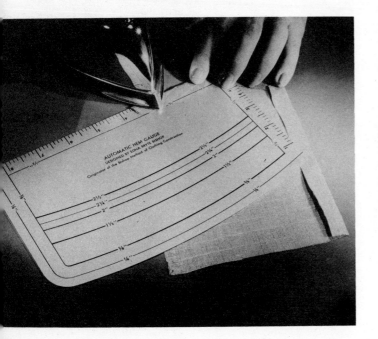

## Pocket unit

When there is only one pocket, place it on the left side of the shirt. Never have a rounded lower edge in the style of the pocket when shirt is made of stripes, plaids, or checks. Turn under seam allowance on three sides of pocket and press.

Turn back and press hem allowance at top. Staystitch raw edge ¼ inch from edge; turn in raw edge on staystitching and press. Stitch hem to pocket along lower edge or slipstitch by hand.

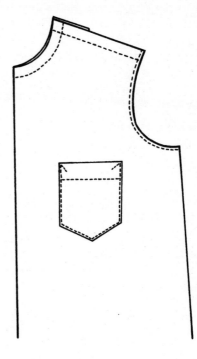

Apply pocket to shirt by stitching close to edge at machine. For reinforcement, at upper corners, stitch back at an angle for ½ inch.

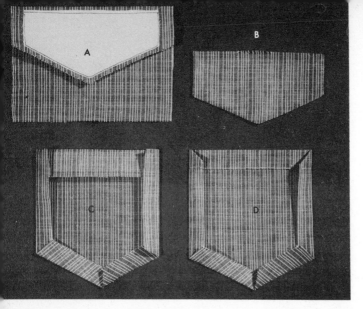

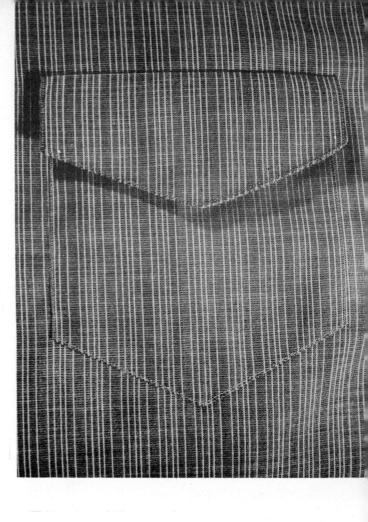

A flap may be added over the pocket.

At A, flap is cut with a fold at the top. Interfacing is stitched inside seamline. With right sides together, stitch around entire flap. Press open one seam edge, and trim double fabric to ¼-inch seam, rounding off seam allowance in corners.

At B, slash fold line for approximately 1½ inches to turn flap. Press and edge-stitch sides and lower edge.

At C, turn in and press seam allowance at sides and lower edge of pocket, and hem allowance at top.

At D, turn under raw edge and stitch hem.

Topstitch pocket to shirt. Reinforce the corners like sketch on page 139. Place right side of flap to right side of shirt above pocket. Stitch along edge and a second row back ¼ inch for reinforcement. Turn down to press in place.

### Complete shirt unit

At shoulders, place outside of yoke facing to inside of shirt front. Stitch together on seamline in direction shown (A).

Turn to inside of yoke facing, and place shoulder edge of yoke to shoulder edge of shirt front, right sides together. Do not pin it, but place edges together gradually as they are stitched. Keep yoke facing side up, and sew through stitching on seamline. It is the same technique as the sleeveless blouse on page 36, *BMCC*. Trim seam to ¼ inch, turn, and press.

Topstitch on yoke close to seam through all thicknesses (B). In plain fabric, make a second row of topstitching ¼ inch from first row.

At armhole, trim seam to point at edges of yoke to eliminate bulk in flat-felled seam (C and C). Staystitch armhole edges together ⅛ inch from edge in direction shown (D).

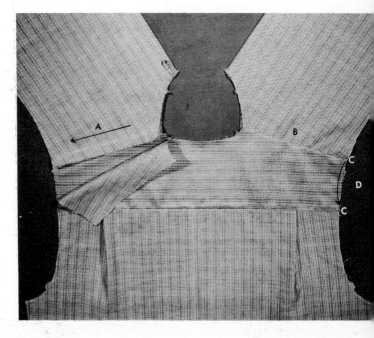

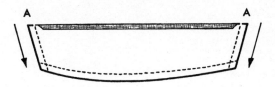

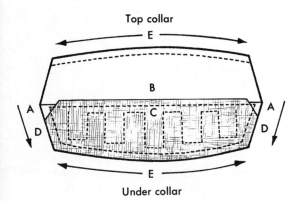

Top collar

Under collar

Place collar right sides together, and stitch ends of collar in direction shown. Trim interfacing to seamline, and cut open fold of collar to seamline at A and A. Press open seam on edge presser; trim away corner, and seam to ¼ inch. Turn and press collar.

### Collar unit

Two other types of collars are shown on pages 150–152 at the end of this chapter.

The collar is always cut lengthwise and on a fold at the outside edge. Press collar in half, right side out.

Cut interfacing identical grain of collar one-half the size of the collar, but wide enough to extend ¼ inch beyond fold line. At corners A and A, cut away interfacing diagonally ¼ inch beyond seamline to eliminate bulk.

Place interfacing toward top collar (B) ¼ inch from fold, but stitch on under collar (C) ⅛ inch from fold. This technique gives support to the folded edge of the collar. Staystitch ends of collar (D and D) on seamline in direction shown. Staystitch neck edges (E and E) just outside seamline in direction shown.

Stitch a design on grain of under collar as shown. This stitching will hold together interfacing and under collar, and will enable collar to launder better and to roll more favorably.

Make a strip of bias tubing to finish ⅛ inch wide (see page 193, *BMCC*); stitch on left edge of shirt front for button loop.

Clip neck edge of shirt at intervals almost to staystitching to give a straighter line for stitching (A). Key and pin center back of under collar to center back of shirt, and ends of collar to center fronts of shirt. With shirt side up, stitch under collar to shirt from notch to notch, approximately one inch from ends of collar (B).

Key raw edge of top collar to raw edge of under collar, and sew to shirt just outside seamline from edge of collar (A) to yoke seam (B).

Clip facings at intervals almost to staystitching to give a straighter line for stitching. Place facings on top collar, right sides together; with shirt side up, stitch through all thicknesses to top of facings (A) on stitching on seamline. Trim all of the collar seams to ¼ inch, and clip curves where necessary. Clip into under collar seam at edge of facings (B). Across back of shirt, turn under collar seam (C) up into collar and press.

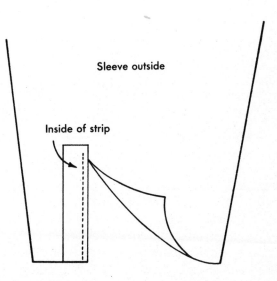

Clip to seamline on top collar at ends of front facings (A). Turn under top collar on seamline and topstitch to seamline of under collar (B).

Stitch edges of facings to shirt with a hand stitch (C) or from outside of garment, stitch facing through well of yoke seam. Press collar.

The shirt collar technique has been simplified here for first learnings on shirts. For a regulation tailored shirt, use the collar technique on pages 104–105, *BMCC*.

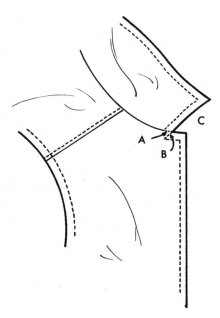

## Cuff and sleeve unit

The placket opening in the sleeve is made exactly as in the photograph and directions at the top left of page 108, *BMCC*. It was used in the shirt in the photograph at the beginning of the chapter. However, in a fine, dressy broadcloth shirt, for example, the following separate facing technique is used.

Slash opening on true grain of fabric. On narrow side of sleeve, sew on a straight strip of fabric, 1½ inches wide and ¾ inch longer than opening. Have right side of strip to right side of sleeve; stitch ¼ inch from edge and ¼ inch above slash.

Topstitch fronts and collar of shirt ¼ to ⅜ inch from edge. Some fabrics, such as gabardine and flannel, are hand-picked.

Topstitching is continuous at corners of collar and facings. Topstitching at A sinks into well of seamline. At B, it is done with same angle as edge of collar (C).

Sleeve outside

Inside of strip

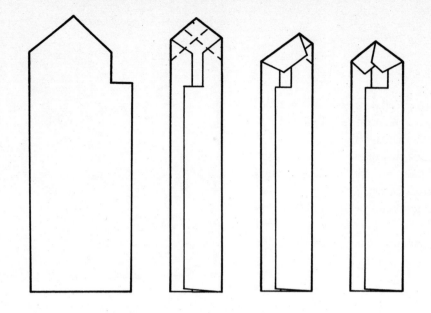

Turn under seam allowance on sleeve facing piece and press. Also, fold and press facing piece on pattern marking line.

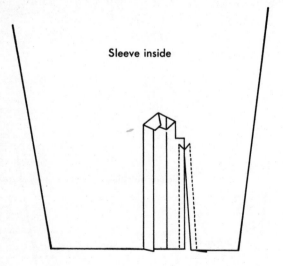

Sleeve inside

Turn in and press ¼ inch on long raw edge of strip. Turn the strip over the slash, lap over first stitching line, and topstitch strip in place on underside. Strip will finish ½ inch wide. Bring sleeve facing piece to right side of sleeve and press in place.

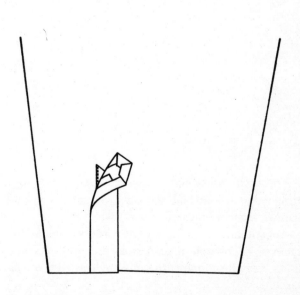

On wide side of sleeve, sew on sleeve facing piece. Have right side of facing piece to inside of sleeve. Stitch ¼ inch from edge and ¼ inch above slash.

Clip to stitching at top of slash, forming a triangle. Press seam on strip toward strip, and press open the seam on the facing piece.

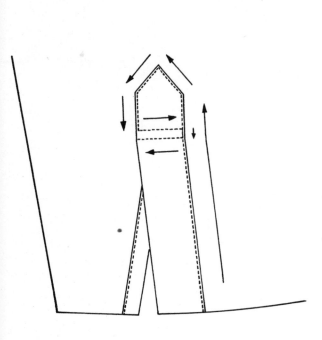

Beginning at sleeve edge, topstitch the side edge of facing piece, point, and back and forth across the top of the opening to conceal and strengthen it.

This photograph shows the finished sleeve opening.

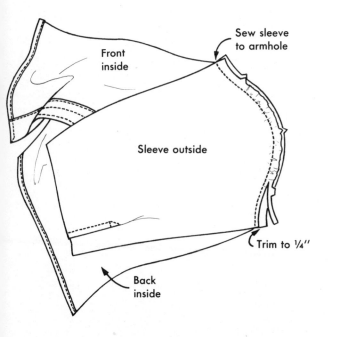

Place inside of sleeve to inside of shirt, and with the sleeve side up, sew sleeve to armhole, easing in sleeve between notches. It is easier to stitch with the outside curve (sleeve) turned up.

Trim only seam of sleeve to ¼ inch. Turn under the shirt seam, clipping staystitching where necessary in curves.

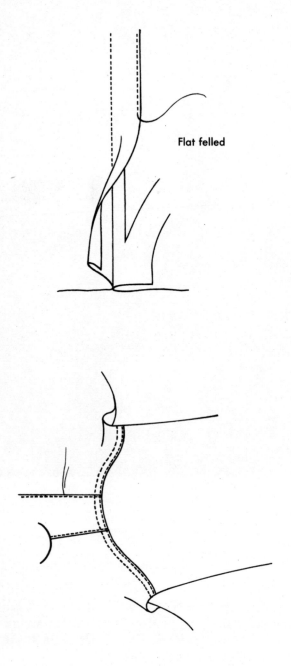

**Flat felled**

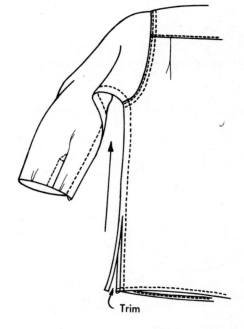

**Trim**

shirt up. Have shirt wrong side out so that you can sew into sleeves, just as you work up your hosiery on your hands before putting them on.

For the man who is small in the waist, some shaping may be desirable at the sides of the shirt, and the shirt could be tapered in cutting before the side seams are stitched.

Pull fabric apart with both hands and both wrists to be sure the seam is smooth underneath, and stitch shirt seam to sleeve to make flat-felled seam.

With wrong sides together, stitch side seams and seams of sleeve from the bottom of shirt up. Trim only back seam of shirt and sleeve to ¼ inch. Turn under the front seam and sew flat-felled seams on both sides of shirt and both sleeves from bottom of

For the man who is large in the waist, it may be desirable to gradually cut on extra at the side seams at the waistline.

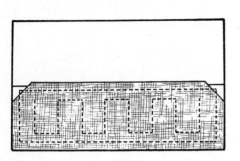

Cuff

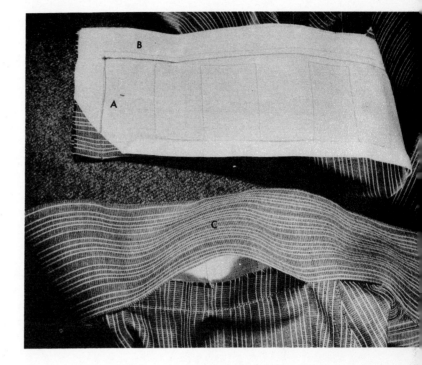

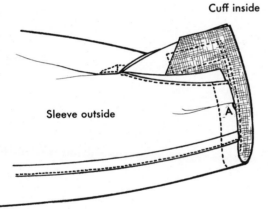

Cuff inside

Sleeve outside

The cuffs are always cut lengthwise and on a fold at the outside edge (unless a curved style, etc.). Press cuff in half right side out. Cut interfacing identical grain of cuff one-half the size of the cuff, but wide enough to extend ¼ inch beyond fold line. The cuffs are made precisely like the collar (pages 141–143), including the stitching design with interfacing and under cuff, except that the ends are not stitched together.

To put on the cuffs, place right side of under cuff to wrong side of sleeve. The edges of the sleeve opening will come to seamline at ends of cuff. Any excess sleeve is laid into pleats that are turned toward sleeve and placed near opening (A). Sew with sleeve side up.

Turn ends of cuff right sides together and stitch ends of cuff through staystitching on seamline (A). Continue to sew across top of cuff for one inch through under cuff stitching on seamline (B). Trim interfacing to seamline and seam to ¼ inch; trim away all of seam across corner.

Turn cuff right side out and press (C).

Topstitch close to edge across top of cuff. At corners, stitch back at an angle as shown so that sides and lower edge of cuff can be topstitched ¼ or ⅜ inch from edge, like collar and shirt fronts. If shirt is hand-picked, hand-pick cuffs, also. Finish cuff with a button and buttonhole. See photograph at beginning of the chapter.

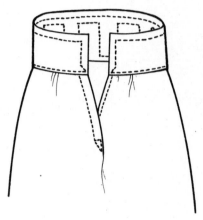

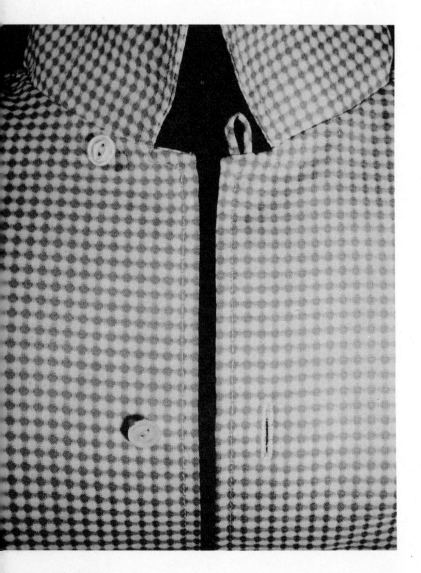

### Complete shirt unit

Normally, buttonholes are made lengthwise for men and boys, and crosswise for women. If there is a box plait on a woman's shirt, then the buttonholes are made lengthwise. Women's shirts button right over left, but men's shirts button left over right.

Do not make a buttonhole near the neckline of sports shirts for men and boys. The bias loop and small button used with it are all that are needed to hold collar in place at the neckline.

Sew on buttons (pages 84–85, *BMCC*).

Final-press shirt (Chapter 9, *BMCC*).

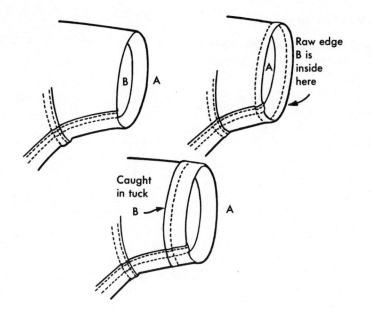

## Short sleeve finish

Turn under and press a hem allowance of 1¼ or 1½ inches (A to B).   Turn up hem a second time and press on raw edge of first turn.

On outside of shirt, stitch a ¼- or ⅜-inch tuck at top of hem, catching raw edge in stitching.   Press tuck up from lower edge.

This is frequently done to shirts when children have outgrown the long sleeves.

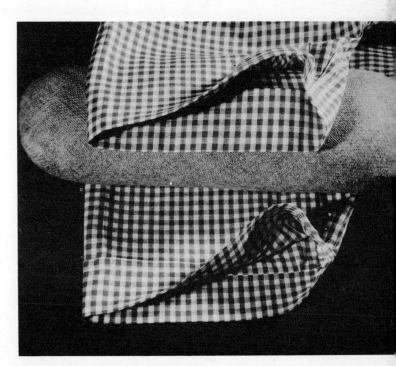

### Collar with neckband cut in one

Place interfacing on inside of top collar, and stay-stitch all edges together ⅝ inch from edge, except A, which is just outside seamline.

Make a row of stitching on fold line of collar (B), and three rows below fold line, ¼ inch apart, beginning and ending at the notches (C). These four rows will be continuous, as sketch illustrates.

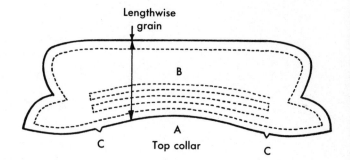

Staystitch edge A of under collar just outside seamline.

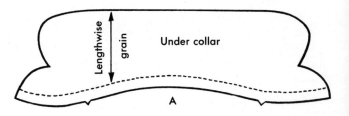

With top collar side turned up, sew on under collar. Trim interfacing to seamline, and seam to scant ¼ inch. Clip into machine stitching at B and C. Clip curves and understitch under collar from D to E, unless entire collar (depending upon fabric) will take topstitching. Turn and press collar.

Stitch through top and under collar on fold line (F).

Collar is put on shirt same as one with separate neckband to follow.

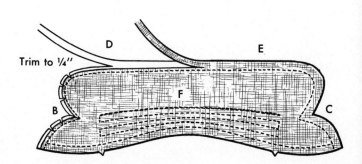

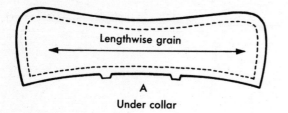

Lengthwise grain

A

Under collar

## Collar with separate neckband

Staystitch interfacing to inside of under collar on seamline, except edge A, which is staystitched just outside seamline.

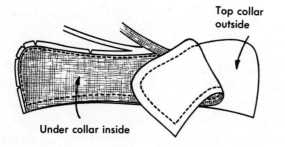

Top collar outside

Under collar inside

With right sides together and under collar turned up, sew on top collar. Stitch through staystitching on seamline. Trim away interfacing to seamline, and seam to scant ¼ inch. Clip curves, turn, and press.

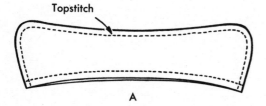

Topstitch

A

On under collar, trim interfacing away to stay-stitching at A, and stitch together raw edges of top and under collar just outside seamline at A. Top-stitch or hand-pick collar.

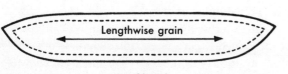

Lengthwise grain

Neckband

Staystitch interfacing to inside of top neckband just outside seamline.

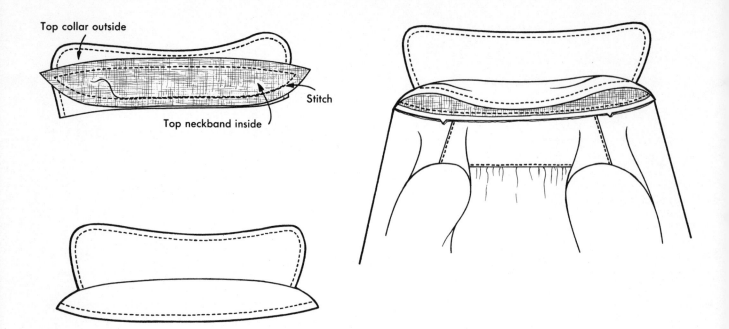

Top collar outside

Stitch

Top neckband inside

Place top neckband to top collar, right sides together, and with outside curve on top (neckband), stitch band to collar.

Staystitch neck edge of under neckband just outside seamline. Place under neckband to under collar, right sides together, and with top neckband turned up, stitch through same stitching on seamline. Trim interfacing to seamline, and seam to scant ¼ inch, Turn and press collar.

The front facing is pressed in place on the inside of the shirt front. Staystitch facing and shirt together at the neckline just outside the seamline. At shoulder edge, sew facing to shoulder seam of shirt. (If the shirt has a yoke, shoulder edge of facing can be included in the yoke seam, as in bottom photo, page 105, *BMCC.*)

Place right side of top neckband to inside of shirt. With shirt side up, sew top neckband to shirt with a ⅝-inch seam.

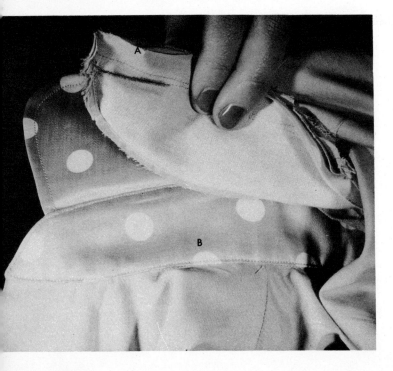

Turn and place raw edge of under neckband to meet raw edge of shirt, right sides together. With top neckband turned up, stitch through stitching on seamline for one inch from edge of collar (A). Repeat on second shirt front.

Trim interfacing to seamline and all of seam to scant ¼ inch. Turn neckband right side out. Press seam up toward neckband. Turn in seam allowance on remainder of under neckband. Edge-stitch opening at machine and continue all around neckband (B).

# Chapter 11

# Vests for men and boys

A. Red Tweed Vest

C. Scotch-Plaid Tweed Vest in Multi-colored Stripes

B. Striped Flannel Vest

D. Necktie Silk Vest

What husband, what son, what man wouldn't enjoy a classic, well-tailored vest made by you? Choose tweed, plaid, wool flannel (a bright color such as red with brass buttons is always a favorite), or linen for daytime wear or spectator sportswear. Wool flannel is preferred over corduroy, because corduroy does not tailor as satisfactorily. Choose a dressier fabric such as tie silk for evening wear.

A luxury lining such as suracel, rayon twill, satin, peau de soie, or taffeta is desirable.

The entire front is interfaced with firm siri, hair canvas, or Formite, depending upon chosen vest fabric.

To buy the pattern in the correct size, choose one comparable to the size purchased in ready-to-wear.

You will find as you make this vest by the Bishop method that you are using the same basic principles you learned on other garments. Also, unit construction carries over in making every garment. Let us see how our principles are applied now in making a vest.

## Front unit

Interfacing for the vest front is cut precisely like pattern for vest front. With tracing paper and tracing wheel, mark pockets on interfacing only.

Staystitch in correct direction of grain all around vest front just outside seamline, except edges A and B, which are staystitched exactly on seamline.

If hair canvas is used as interfacing in front of vest, then a piece of muslin will have to be cut and applied to edges A and B (pages 152–153, *The Bishop Method of Clothing Construction*°). With small stitches, staystitch ½ inch each side of corner (C) on seamline.

With contrasting thread, baste-stitch pocket location and size lines through both layers of fabric. Unless four pockets are preferred, mark lower pocket on right front, and upper and lower pockets on left front.

Make regulation welt pockets (pages 174–176, *BMCC*). It is important to remember welts are always made of a lengthwise piece of fabric, and the back pocket piece must be identical to the grain of garment. The front pocket piece is cut of lining and is crosswise grain. The slot pocket on pages 145–146, *BMCC*, may also be used on vests.

°Hereafter referred to as *BMCC*.

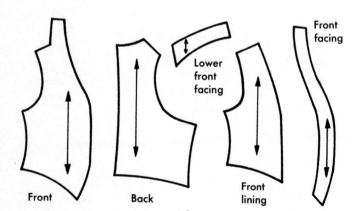

Front

Back

Lower front facing

Front lining

Front facing

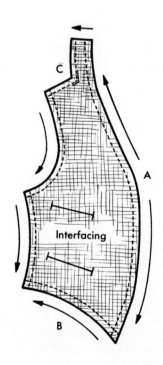

Interfacing

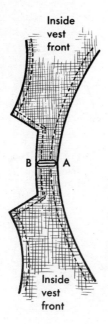

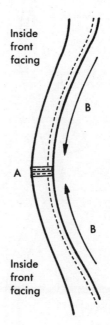

Stitch center back seam of 2 vest fronts. Trim away interfacing to seamline, press open vest seam, and trim to ¼ inch. Beginning 1 inch from edge, trim seam away diagonally to ⅛ inch at A and B to eliminate bulk at seamline.

Stitch center back seam of front facings and press open (A). Topstitch each side of seam, and trim away all of seam up to topstitching.

Facing will be stitched to vest in next step with vest side up. To keep edge grain perfect, staystitch off-grain edge B of facing *at neckline only*, just outside seamline.

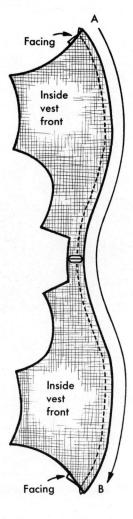

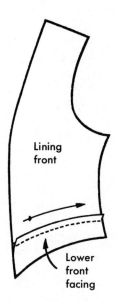

Stitch lower front facing to bottom edge of lining front in direction shown. Press seam up; leave wool seam ⅝ inch and trim lining seam to ⅜ inch.

With right side of facings and vest fronts placed together, and with vest side up, sew facing to vest fronts through staystitching on seamline all the way from one lower front edge (A) to the other (B). Use smallest stitch at machine for a distance of one inch at lower edges.

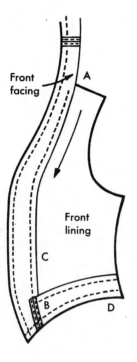

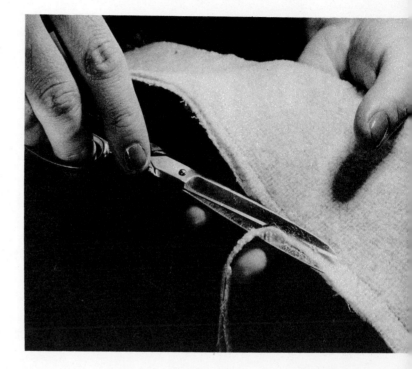

Beginning one inch from top of lining front at A, stitch inside edge of front facing to lining front and lower facing. At B, press open seam, topstitch each side of it, and trim away all of seam up to topstitching. Press remainder of seam (C) toward lining front. Leave wool seam ⅝ inch and trim lining seam to ⅜ inch.

With right sides together and with vest side up, sew lower facings (D) to vest fronts through staystitching on seamline. Use smallest stitch at machine for a distance of one inch at front corner.

At front and bottom edges of vest, trim interfacing to seamline. Then, hold scissors perfectly flat for trimming, and stagger both seam edges of vest at once, making one toward top of vest ¼ inch and under one ⅛ inch. Round off seam allowance at corners to within a few threads of stitching line.

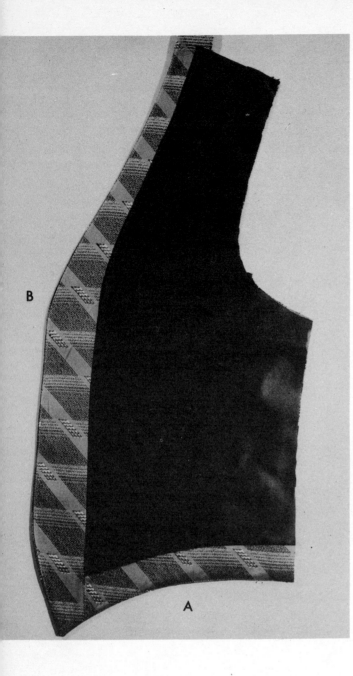

Turn vest right side out. Understitch bottom edge (A), beginning in corners as far as possible to one inch from side edge of vest. Understitch front edges of vest (B), also going into corners as far as possible. Understitching is a row of machine stitching along the edge of the facing that catches the two trimmed seams to the facing. Press edge from top side of vest.

Place right sides together and stitch lining front to vest front at armhole in correct direction of grain. Trim away interfacing to seamline and lining and vest fabric to ¼ inch. At intervals, clip curved armhole seam to seamline. Turn right side out, and beginning as far up armhole as possible, understitch armhole seam to side edge. Press armhole edge from top side of vest.

This photograph shows the completed front unit from the top side.

## Back lining unit

Stitch center back seam of upper back lining and under back lining in direction shown and press open seams. Staystitch neckline, shoulders, armholes, and sides just outside seamline in direction shown.

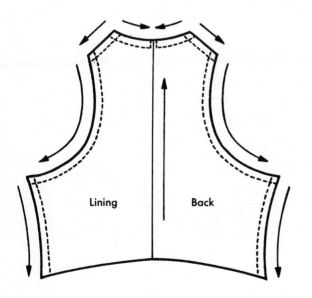

Then, place lining backs right sides together, and stitch armholes (A and A) and lower edge (B) in direction shown. Trim A and B seams to ¼ inch, and clip curves of armholes. Understitch lower edge, beginning and ending one inch from side edges. Turn right side out and press from topside of lining. Instead of understitching armholes as front ones were done, topstitch them close to edge for added strength, *after* vest is completed.

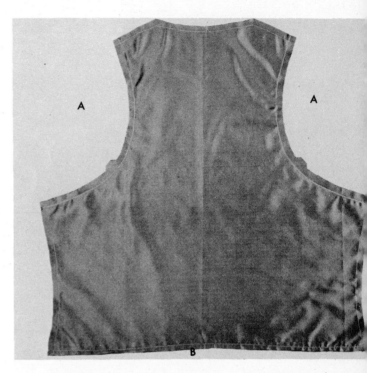

## Complete vest unit

Clip corner (A) on shoulder of vest front up to staystitching on seamline. Open up shoulders, and pin and stitch right side of lining front to right side of under lining, and on around to right side of vest to right side of upper lining. Continue across neckline, joining vest front and upper lining; do second shoulder seam same as first. Sew with vest side up and use short stitches in corners. Open up armhole seams when stitching over them.

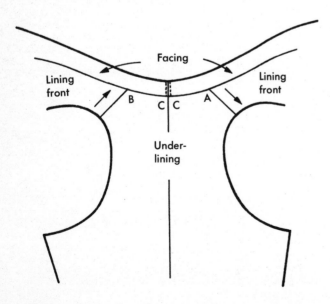

Stitching will begin at A, and continue around to B. The only part that will not be stitched at the machine is neck edge (C) of under lining and facing.

Trim away shoulder seams diagonally as shown at A and A. Trim all of seam to ¼ inch and press down toward back lining.

Whipstitch back lining to neck facing by hand. (This technique is the same as the blouse, dress, or jumper with neck and armhole facing cut in one (pages 35–36, BMCC).

Turn lining wrong side out, and at the side seams, place right side of vest to right side of upper lining, and right side of lining in front vest to right side of under lining. With a continuous line of stitching and a ⅝-inch seam, stitch a complete circle. Turn right side out, after clipping seam to a point at armhole and lower edges. Press seam toward back of vest.

Repeat for second side, except an opening must be left in the middle third of under lining to turn right side out (A to B). Whipstitch same as neck edge. Topstitch back armholes close to edge for added strength.

Make 4 or 5 keyhole buttonholes in left front no longer than ⅝ inch. The vest will not be complete until it has had a professional pressing (Chapter 9, *BMCC*). Sew buttons on right front with a shank (pages 84–85, *BMCC*).

# Slacks for men and boys

Many of the techniques for men's or boys' slacks are identical to those for women's. Even in fitting them with perfection, it is just as important to have the grain evenly balanced on the figure. Slacks do not take much time to make—cut out several pair before you go to the machine to begin to sew. These techniques are used on boys' slacks, beginning with school age. It is assuredly a place where you can save much money in the family budget, and moreover, have slacks with a handsome, quality look.

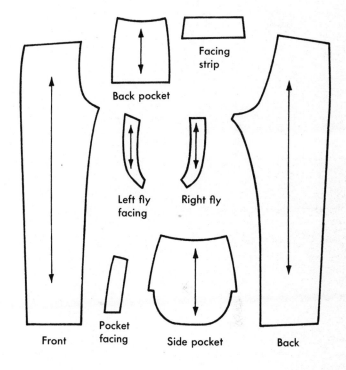

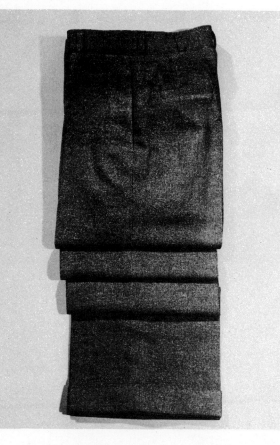

Make them in flannel, sharkskin, whipcord, corduroy, wide whale cotton, wash-and-wear fabrics, or other desirable ones of your family's choice.

Buy the slacks pattern by the waist measurement.

### Back unit

Sometimes, the front of the slacks may need to be increased in width for the individual figure and not the back; or the reverse may occur, the back will need to be increased and not the front.

Staystitch top of slacks and sides for a depth of ten inches just outside seamline, and in correct direction shown.

To make creases in slacks, on underside mark crease line on one layer of fabric only, with tracing paper and wheel. Through both layers of fabric, place 4 or 5 pins in marking line.

Turn back and press top layer on pin line. Remove pins. The crease begins 8 inches below waistline on back of slacks.

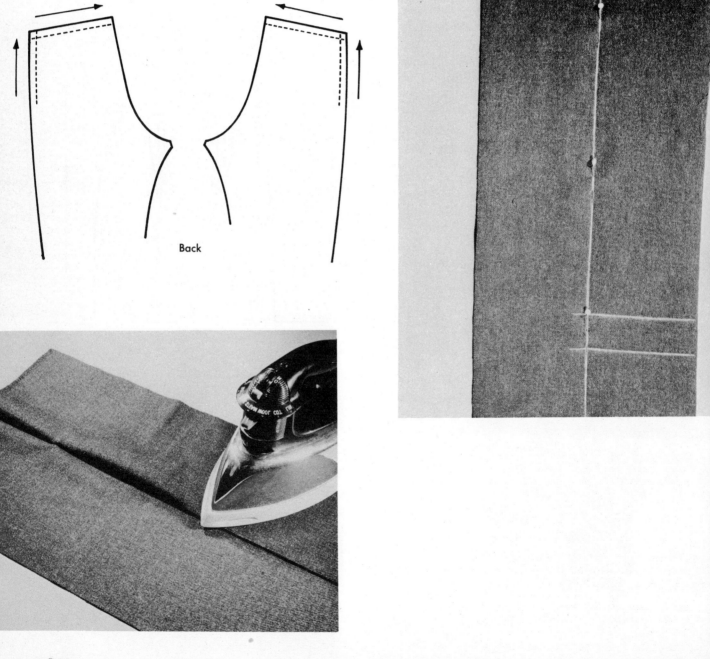

Back

Turn fabric to have under layer on top now. Fold back top layer to meet under crease and press second side.

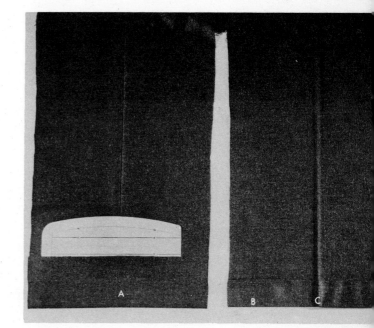

Turn up hem at lower edge to underside and press (A). Then, turn up cuff on cuff line and press (B). Finally, fold and press crease line again at lower edge to restore it (C).

Sew seam at crotch in direction shown. Considerable strain is placed on this seam; strengthen it by stitching with machine set one point or even less to zigzag. If you do not have a zigzag machine, sew with shortest stitch at machine.

Set the machine more than one point to zigzag and stitch both sides of seam ¼ inch from edge. Stretch seam in curve only. If you do not have a zigzag machine, staystitch seam, and stretch in curved area, also. Press open seam.

Stitch darts and press toward center back.

Inside back

### Back pocket

If you just make one pocket on the back, have it on the left side. You may need to straighten location line for pocket (A) after the dart is stitched. B is the newly drawn pocket location line.

This pocket uses many of the steps from the modulated welt pocket, pages 116–117, *The Bishop Method of Clothing Construction.* [*]

Mark pocket location lines and size lines on muslin pocket pieces (1 and 2).

To make the welt, tear or cut a lengthwise strip of fabric 1½ inches wide and as long as pocket piece is wide (A to B). Fold welt lengthwise (C), wrong sides together; press; and stitch along the edge, allowing ¼-inch seam. Welt will finish ½ inch wide.

If the little tab is desired coming out of top of pocket (see photograph on page 168), make it double of slacks fabric, turn, and press. Leave open D edge to turn right side out.

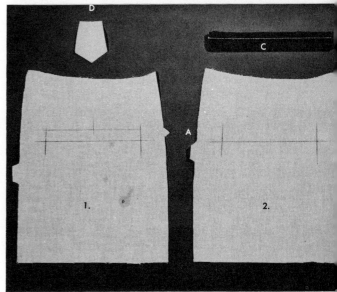

Stitch facing strips to pocket marking lines ¼ inch from raw edge of facing strips (A and A).

Staystitch lower edges of facing strips (B and B) ¼ inch from edge. Turn under ¼ inch to staystitching and press; topstitch to muslin pocket pieces.

Then, sew on welt (C) through same stitching ¼ inch from edge. Stitching *must not* extend beyond pocket size lines. If tab is being used, stitch in place ¼ inch from edge also (D).

Trim away muslin pocket piece above raw edges of welt (E) on this section *only*.

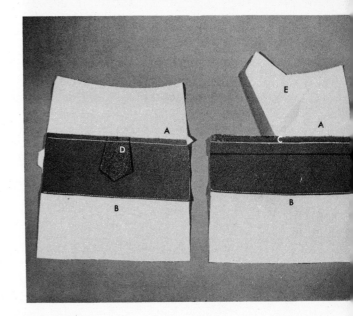

* Hereafter referred to as *BMCC*.

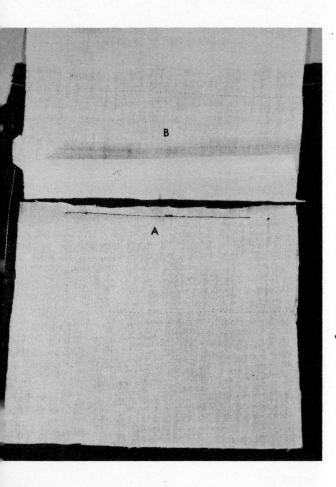

Place raw edges of welt to pocket marking line on right side of slacks, and with welt side down, sew on welt through previous stitching to *size lines only* (A).

Key raw edge of facing strip on second pocket piece to pocket marking line on right side of slacks, and with tab turned down, sew on second pocket piece through previous stitching to size lines only (B). The muslin was rolled up for the photograph to show lower pocket piece, but will be out flat for stitching. Check for accuracy. The stitching lines should be ½ inch apart and must end at the size lines.

Remove baste-stitching at location and size lines in slacks. On inside of slacks, starting at center, slash between stitching lines and diagonally to corners, leaving triangles ½ inch long at ends of opening. Turn pocket sections to inside; press pocket. Welt will fit with perfection in opening.

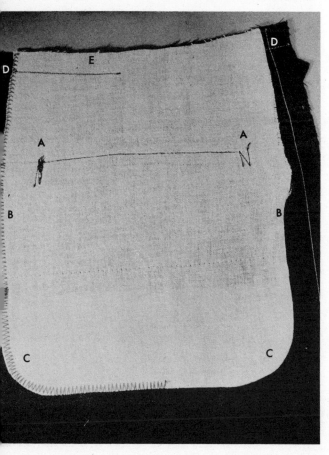

Stitch the triangle to the pocket sections, going back and forth many times to fasten securely. This connecting line at base of triangles (A and A) also squares the ends of the pocket.

Trim any uneven edges that do not fit together with perfection. With wrong sides together, stitch sides and bottom in ¼-inch seam, going up sides as far as possible (B and B). Round off corners in stitching and trim them away (C and C).

Turn pocket pieces and press edges. Zigzag edges of pocket, going all the way to the top of it (D and D). Turn under single raw edge ¼ inch as you zigzag above B and B. Trim away ¼ inch on welt; it must not be turned in at that area. Stitch muslin pocket in place at top of slacks (E).

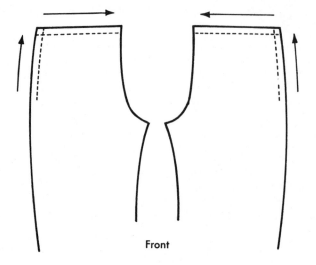

Front

This is the completed pocket. For security reasons, there would be a buttonhole in the tab, and the button would be sewn on the trousers.

Without the tab, the button and buttonhole are optional. Yet, it is preferred to lock in the wallet.

## Front unit

Staystitch top of slacks and sides for a depth of ten inches just outside seamline in correct direction shown.

Make creases and cuffs in slacks the same as you learned with back unit on pages 164–165.

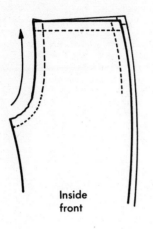

Inside
front

Sew seam at crotch in direction shown. It will be permanent stitching up to the metal on the zipper; lockstitch threads, and then baste-stitch seam for length of metal part of zipper plus all of the tape at the top. Special trousers' zippers are available.

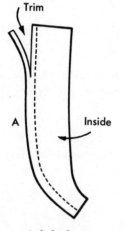

Trim

A

Inside

Left fly facing

On left front fly facing, at edge A, stitch on a piece of lightweight fabric cut same as facing. Trim seam to scant ¼ inch; turn and press.

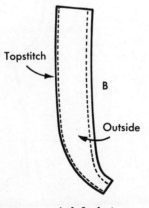

Topstitch

B

Outside

Left fly facing

Topstitch close to edge for added strength. Stitch together raw edges at B.

The entire fly is made in such a way that you just work with the two parts of the center front seam in following these steps.

On left front, place edge B of facing to meet raw edge of left front seam, right sides together.

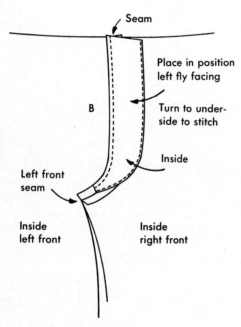

Turn to underside of left front seam and sew on facing as near basting line as possible.

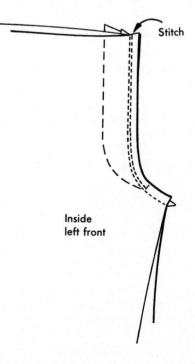

Stagger edges in trimming and understitch edge of facing. Photograph illustrates steps to this point.

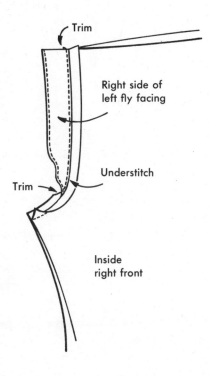

Trim

Right side of
left fly facing

Understitch

Trim

Inside
right front

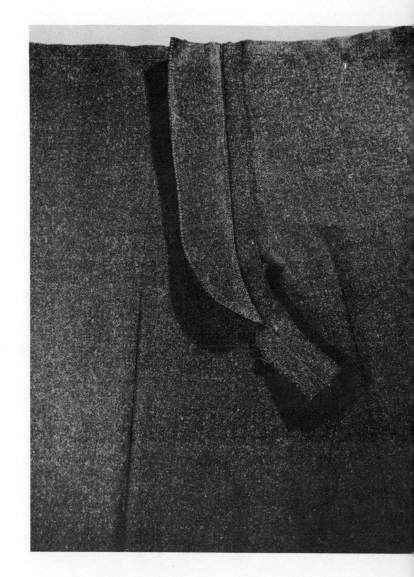

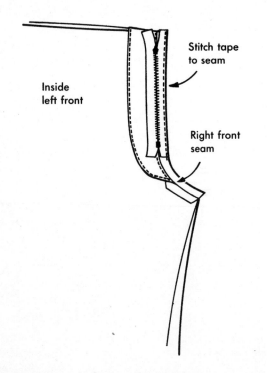

Inside
left front

Stitch tape
to seam

Right front
seam

A

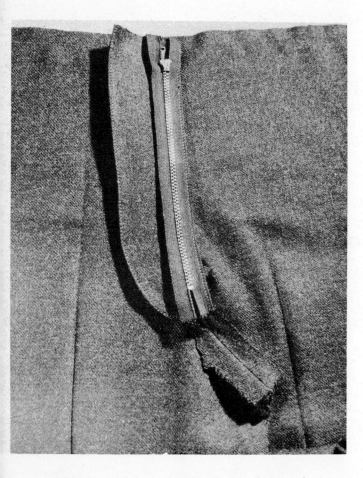

With right side of zipper to right side of right front seam, sew zipper to seam from top down to lower edge. Key edge of zipper tape to edge of seam, and with regular presser foot, stitch close to edge, having edges of tape and seam in middle of right side of presser foot (A).

The photograph illustrates this step.

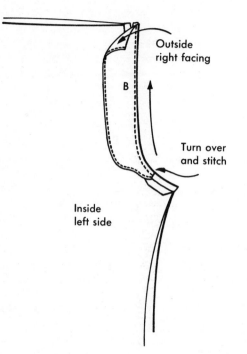

Outside
right facing

B

Turn over
and stitch

Inside
left side

Make right fly exactly as you made left fly facing.

Place right side of facing (edge B) to meet edge of zipper tape. Turn and have underside of right front seam on top, and stitch from bottom up near same line of stitching that sewed on zipper tape.

Turn zipper right side up, roll right front seam up to chain, and with zipper foot, sew close to zipper chain on right front seam. The right facing is out flat.

The photograph shows this step completed.

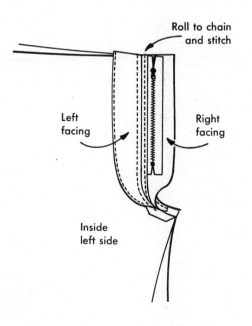

Roll to chain
and stitch

Left
facing

Right
facing

Inside
left side

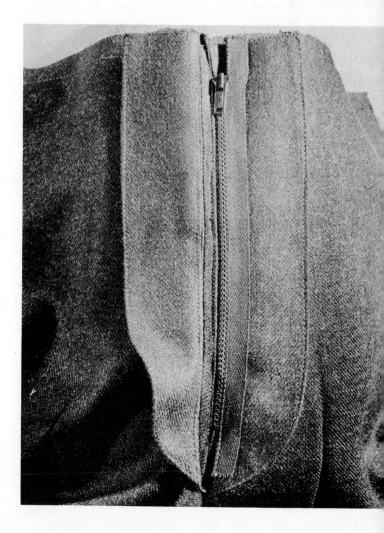

Lay zipper flat toward left front of slacks. Press flat on underside and topside of slacks at seamline. Pin zipper tape to left front fly facing. From bottom up, stitch close to edge of zipper tape with regular presser foot. Put on zipper foot and make a second row of stitching close to metal chain.

Note the photograph of this completed step.

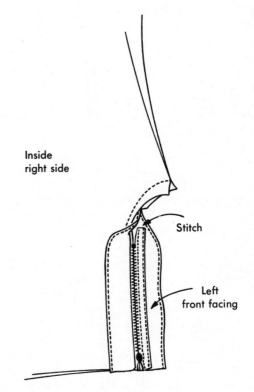

Inside right side

Stitch

Left front facing

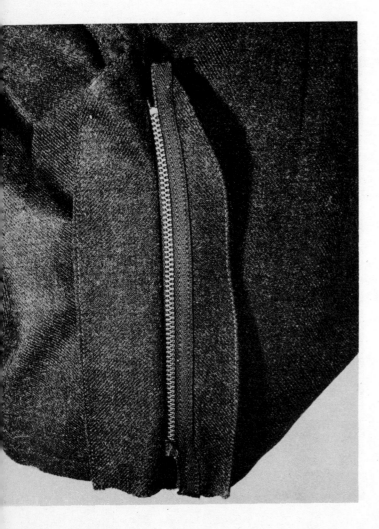

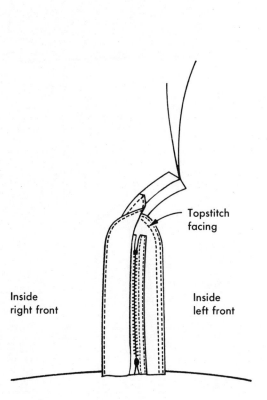

Inside right front

Inside left front

Topstitch facing

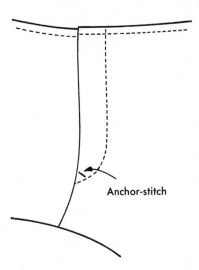

Anchor-stitch

Anchor-stitch at an angle for ⅝ inch at lower edge of opening. Use zigzag stitch at machine. If you do not have a zigzag machine, stitch back and forth several times to anchor.

Turn to underside of right front seam to remove baste-stitching.

On left front, topstitch facing to trousers. Stitch from bottom up ½ inch from edge of facing.

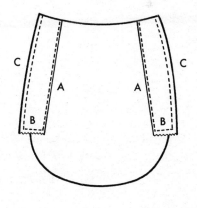

## Side pockets unit

On pocket facings, turn in ¼ inch on edge A and press. Pink edge B. Key raw edge of pocket facing at C to raw edge of muslin pocket. Stitch raw edges in place at B and C ¼ inch from edge. Close to the edge, topstitch edge A to muslin pocket.

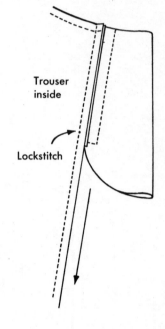

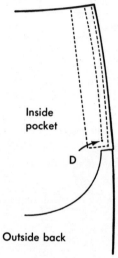

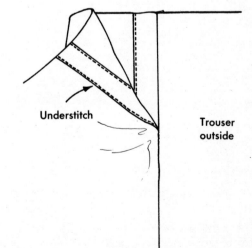

With right side of muslin pocket facing right side of the back of the slacks, sew pocket to slacks with pocket side up. End stitching ⅝ inch from lower edge of pocket (D), and lockstitch threads securely. Repeat for second pocket.

Then, do this same step and sew pockets to front of slacks.

Key together lockstitching on side front and side back of slacks. Beginning at lockstitching, close side seams, stitching down to bottom of slacks.

On front of slacks, trim away muslin close to seamline at pocket edge. Stagger edges of slacks' seam and understitch (see photograph of vest, page 157).

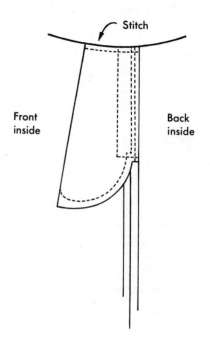

Stitch

Front
inside

Back
inside

Match upper edges with upper edge of slacks, and
stitch together.

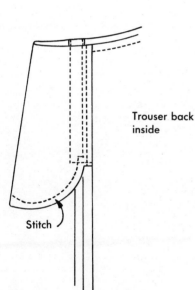

Trouser back
inside

Stitch

On back of slacks, press pocket seam toward back
of trousers.

Below pocket, press open seam.

Key together lockstitching at lower edge of pockets,
and beginning exactly at lockstitching, close pocket
pieces to waist edges. Round off any corners to keep
out lint.

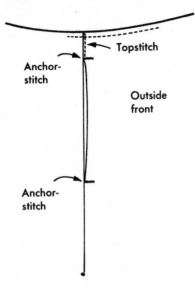

Anchor-stitch straight across for ½ inch at lower edge of pocket opening and 1⅝ inches from top. Topstitch pocket close to edge from upper anchor to top of slacks.

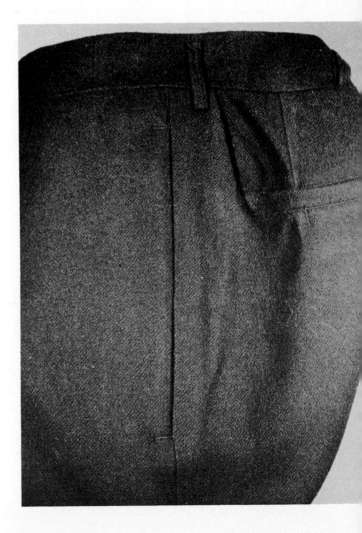

This photograph shows a finished pocket on the completed slacks.

## Band unit

Always make straps from a lengthwise strip of fabric ¾ inch wide, having one edge on the selvage. Press back raw edge ¼ inch and press selvage over it ¼ inch. This makes straps ¼ inch wide. Stitch at machine through center of strap.

Place straps around top of slacks where desired, and stitch to raw edge (A). The underside of the strap is placed to the right side of the slacks.

The band to finish 1½ inches wide is cut of a lengthwise strip 2¾ inches wide and 3½ inches longer than waist measurement.

Interfacing of muslin is also lengthwise and as long as the band, but is only 2 inches wide.

Place interfacing ¼ inch from back raw edge of band, and stitch together near edge of interfacing. Press band, rolling in place from back edge toward front edge.

Roll over ⅝ inch to extend on back of band. Stitch near edge of interfacing wherever it falls on front edge of band.

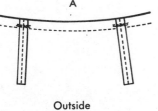

A

Outside
of slacks

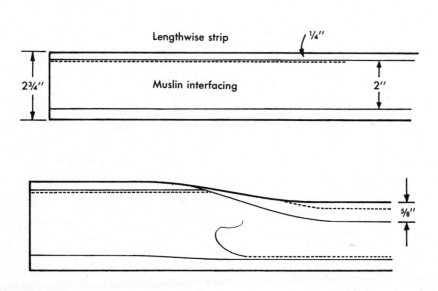

Lengthwise strip     ¼″

2¾″     Muslin interfacing     2″

⅝″

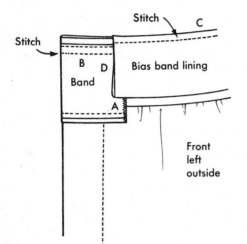

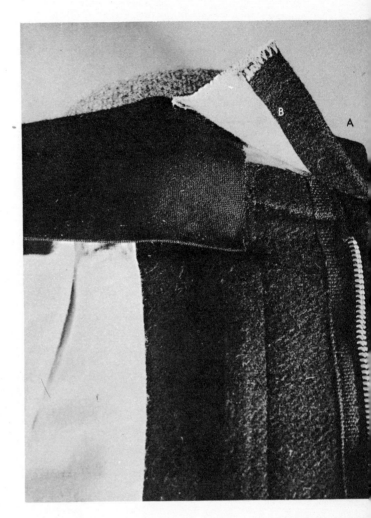

For tolerance needed in slacks, pin band to slacks with the same techniques you learned on the skirt (page 43, *BMCC*). The band extends a seam allowance at right front fly facing, and several inches extra at left front fly facing.

With right sides together, and with band side up, stitch band to top of slacks, catching straps in stitching.

Press open band seam at waistline and trim muslin to seamline from pockets.

At left fly facing, zigzag A edge first. Turn band extension to right side of band and stitch on seamline (B).

Cut bias muslin (or rayon twill in matching color of slacks) 5 inches wide. Press in half and stitch together raw edges ⅜ inch from edge. Place raw edges to meet raw edge of back of band (C). At left front fly facing, lap muslin ½ inch over band extension (D). Beginning at raw edge of band extension and with band on *top*, sew muslin to band ⅜ inch from edge all the way across to raw edge of band at right front fly facing. Turn to inside and press seam down. Muslin will be ¼ inch from top of band.

On band extension, press open top seam on edge presser (A). Stagger width of seam in trimming and round off seam allowance in corner. Turn right side out and press.

Turn under lower edges of band extension and whipstitch by hand to seamline. Raw edges may be staggered first in trimming. At end of extension, clip lower waistline seam up to stitching.

Turn under raw edge of bias (A) and stitch in place. B edge will be held in place with topstitching, as in next photograph.

Continue topstitching on left fly facing to top of band.

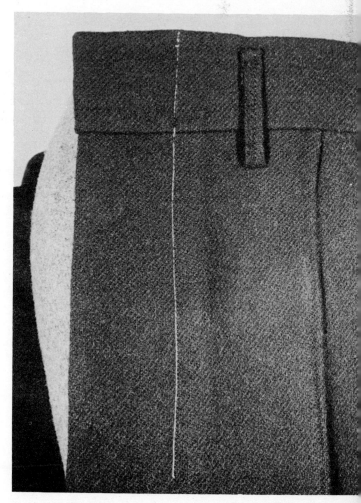

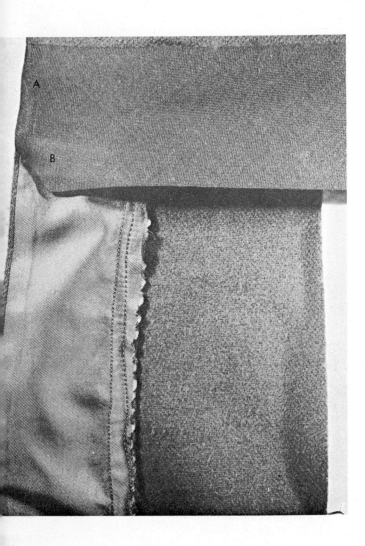

At right front fly facing, turn bias muslin to outside on fold line at top of band. Beginning at edge of facing, sew ends together parallel to edge of facing (A). Use small stitches in the corner for ½ inch. Stagger width of seam in trimming, and round off seam allowance in corner. Turn right side out and press.

Trim away lower part of waistline seam at an angle. Turn in bias muslin diagonally to cover raw edges (B).

Topstitch this edge as shown.

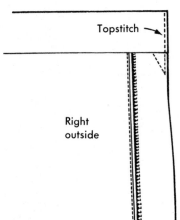

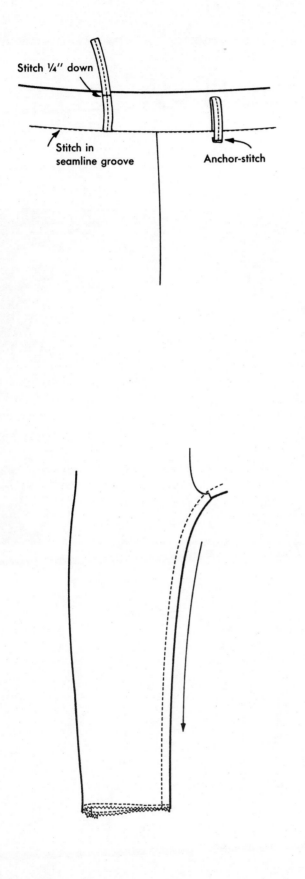

Stitch ¼″ down

Stitch in
seamline groove

Anchor-stitch

With right side of slacks turned up, stitch bias in place at lower edge with a concealed row of stitching in the seamline groove at waistline.

The fold of the bias extends to cover up the raw edge of the waistline seam. Final-press band.

Stitch loops ¼ inch from top edge of band. Fold over and bring ½ inch below waistline seam. Turn under raw edge ¼ inch and anchor-stitch in place. This technique makes two sizes of loops, one for a narrow belt and the other for a wide belt.

Sew on hook and eye (see photograph, page 134).

### Cuff unit

Staystitch raw edge ¼ inch from edge and pink with pinking shears.

Stitch two inside leg seams from the crotch down, and press open. Trim all seams in hem of cuff to ¼ inch, going ⅛ inch beyond fold line of hem (see C in top photograph, page 162, *BMCC*).

Press hem line and cuff line again to restore creases.

Stitch hem in place as shown at the bottom of page 46, *BMCC*.

Hold cuff in place with concealed hand stitching at two seams.

A firm rayon may be stitched into the seams at the knees of slacks to help retain their shape and reduce wear.

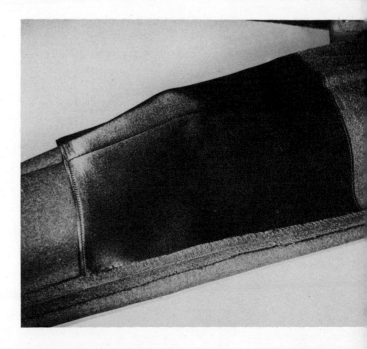

# Sports jackets for men and boys

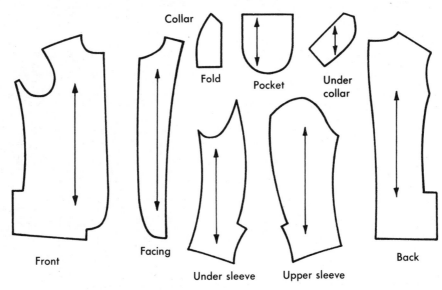

Collar

Fold

Pocket

Under collar

Front

Facing

Under sleeve

Upper sleeve

Back

Making sports jackets for various members of your family will bring you much pleasure and satisfaction. The techniques presented in this chapter will enable you to construct a jacket with high standards and a fine, quality appearance. The learnings will be identical for making men's or boys' topcoats or overcoats. To buy the jacket pattern in the correct size, choose one comparable to the size purchased in ready-to-wear.

## Cutting interfacing

After cutting and marking the fabric for the jacket, remove pattern pieces, and place the sections of the jacket in units of work.

Unless the pattern company has given separate pattern pieces for cutting interfacing *exactly* like the directions to follow, use the original pattern pieces for jacket to cut interfacing. It is always cut on identical grain as jacket.

**Hair canvas or Formite.** Hair canvas was used in the heavier tweed jacket in the photograph, and Formite was used in the lighter weight jacket done in striped flannel.

Interfacing for the front of the jacket is cut two inches wider at the bottom than width of facing (A). Underarm, it is cut to first marking line for dart (B). Cut *unbleached muslin* for remainder of underarm interfacing, beginning at second marking line for dart (C).

To prevent the front of the jacket from breaking at the armhole, cut an extra piece of hair canvas (A) that will be stitched and quilted on front interfacing (see page 194). At B edges, cut ⅞ inch smaller than edge of tissue. If needed, several layers may be used, or Pelomite may be pressed on this piece. Stagger any additional layers in size.

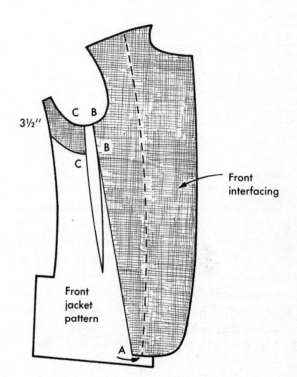

3½″

C  B

B

C

B

A

Front interfacing

Front jacket pattern

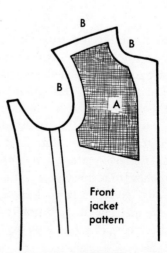

B

B

B

A

Front jacket pattern

The interfacing for the collar is cut from hair canvas or Formite, using the pattern for the under collar. It will be in two pieces and on the bias.

To cut the interfacing for the bottom of the sleeve, see page 200.

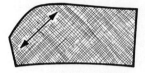

Collar interfacing

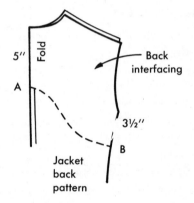

**Unbleached muslin.** To preshrink, see page 11, *The Bishop Method of Clothing Construction.*

Muslin interfacing for the back of the jacket is cut like the back pattern from A (5 inches down center back) to B (3½ inches below armhole). Remove pattern and cut freehand from A to B, as shown with broken line.

Because you have straight of grain, you may cut the muslin on a fold and omit the seam at the center back.

This is especially advisable for heavy fabric. See photograph on page 190 for lightweight fabric.

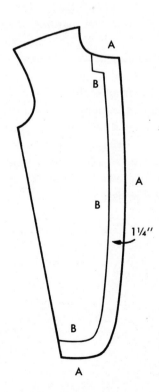

Cut a strip of muslin from front pattern piece on identical grain of jacket front. It is used at the edge where the facing will be attached, and extends to the center front at neckline. This eliminates the hair canvas from the seamline, holds interfacing securely, and makes possible sharp, thin front edges. Place front tissue pattern on identical grain of muslin and cut edges A. Remove pattern. Measure and mark line B, 1¼ inches from front edge A, and cut along B. Unless you have very soft wool, a strip of muslin is not necessary on front edge of Formite interfacing. Staystitch interfacing to garment on seamline at this area.

*Hereafter referred to as *BMCC.*

Enough true bias of muslin 2½ inches wide is needed to cushion the hem of the jacket. When sewing together strips of it, overlap ⅛ inch on true grain, and stitch at machine.

## Cutting lining

It is best to wait to cut the lining until the jacket has been sewn together and tried on for a fitting. If any cutting-to-fit alterations were necessary in cutting out the jacket, cut the lining with the same alterations. Then, if any fitting is necessary when the jacket is tried on, cut and stitch lining with the same alterations.

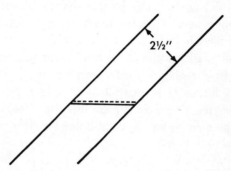

The original pattern used for cutting the garment is preferred for cutting lining. The cutting and fitting alterations are more easily made, and in carrying out special directions below for cutting, the lining will fit the garment with perfection.

Sleeves are cut to the finished length of jacket sleeve plus ¾ inch extra for ease in lining. Omit sleeve pleat. The ¾ inch extra for ease is not necessary on *boys'* jackets.

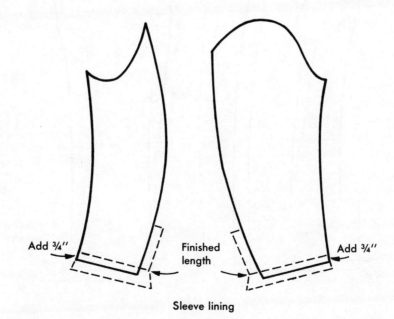

Sleeve lining

The front and back of the lining are cut to the finished length of the jacket plus ¾ inch extra for ease. As above, the ¾ inch extra for ease is not necessary on boys' jackets. The pleat extension at the side opening is needed on the front of the lining, but is cut off back lining.

Chalk mark, on the jacket front tissue pattern, the width front facing will extend on it (line A). Measure 1¼ inches (2 seam widths) from line A toward front of jacket, and chalk mark (line B). Fold under tissue pattern on line B to cut lining for jacket front.

One inch extra width is added at center back of lining down to the waistline for a pleat to give necessary ease. If the back of the jacket is not cut too much off grain, leave edge A on the fold to the waistline, even though the pleat will not be a true one-inch width all the way down.

With the same slope as the shoulder line, cut on 1½ inches of lining at armholes front and back, tapering to ¼ inch extra at notch. Continue to add ¼ inch at armhole from notch to side of jacket.

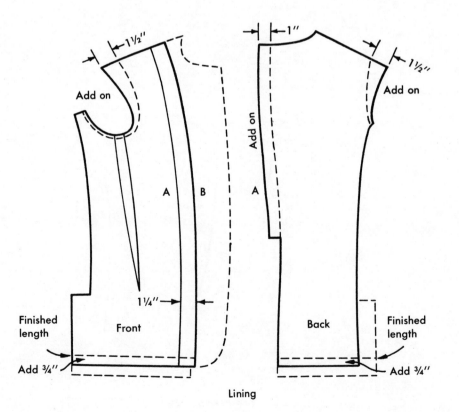

Lining

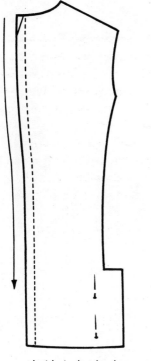

Inside jacket back

## Jacket back unit

For pleat extension, mark pleat line on one piece only. Pin line with two pins through both layers of fabric. Turn back and press top piece of fabric on pin line. Remove pins. Turn over to second piece of fabric. Fold pleat line and key to first piece. Press on second side. See photographs on pages 164–165.

Stitch center back seam on seamline in direction shown, and press open in same direction. Beginning 1¼ inches from neck edge, trim seam away diagonally to ⅛ inch to eliminate bulk at seamline.

Place interfacing next to underside of jacket. Staystitch interfacing to jacket, in direction shown, just outside seamline.

Staystitch lower edge ¼ inch from edge.

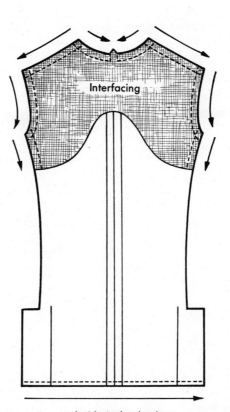

Inside jacket back

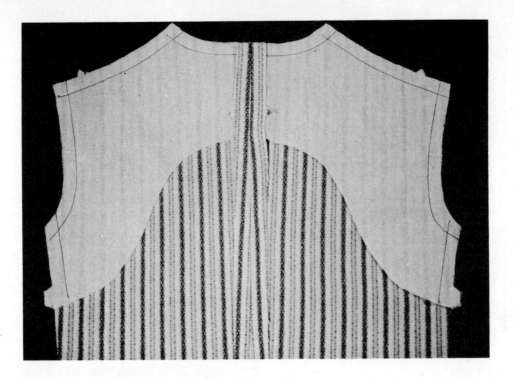

It is advisable to staystitch interfacing in center back seam for support in lightweight fabrics.

Open out pleat extensions. Using automatic hem gauge, turn up hem 1½ inches and press. Turn back pleat extensions again and press to restore pleat line.

Trim center back seam in hem to ¼ inch, going ⅛ inch beyond fold of hem.

Place bias muslin (cut 2½ inches wide) in hem 1 inch from lower edge of jacket. Extend it ½ inch beyond crease line of pleats. At points A, cut away muslin diagonally to remove it ¼ inch from each side of corner of jacket. Stitch muslin in place ¼ inch from edge at sides and lower edge of muslin. Stitching will be ¼ inch from fold lines on jacket.

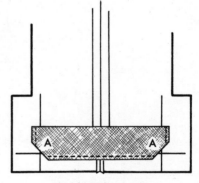

Inside jacket back

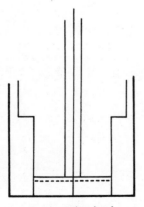

Inside jacket back

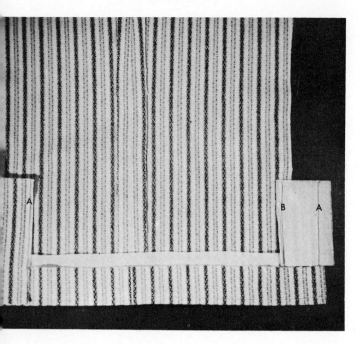

In this lightweight jacket, a straight strip of muslin was also stitched in place at A and B to support open pleat.

Finally, press hem and pleat extensions in place again to restore them.

## Jacket front unit

Stitch dart in jacket front and press toward side. At A, slash dart on fold line for a depth of 1½ inches. Trim under edge away diagonally to ⅛ inch at armhole and upper edge to ⅜ inch. Staystitch lower edge of jacket ¼ inch from edge.

On upper left front, make regulation welt pocket, following directions on pages 174–176, *BMCC*. It is important to remember that the grain of the under pocket piece must match the grain of the jacket front. See jackets in photographs on page 184.

On both jacket fronts, sew on patch pockets, following directions on pages 176–177, *BMCC*. The top pocket is made through the interfacing, but the bottom ones never are.

Following are two additional techniques you may choose to use in making the patch pockets.

In some fabrics, the pocket will be stronger with interfacing across the top.

Press hem allowance in place at top of pocket. Cut a lengthwise strip of hair canvas ¾ inch deeper (A) than width of hem and ¾ inch narrower (B and B) than width of pocket. Place inside hem up to fold line. Open out hem, and stitch interfacing to hem ¼ inch below fold (C). When lining is stitched on pocket edge (D), stitching will catch interfacing here, also. Follow the directions at the top of page 177, *BMCC*, for sewing on lining.

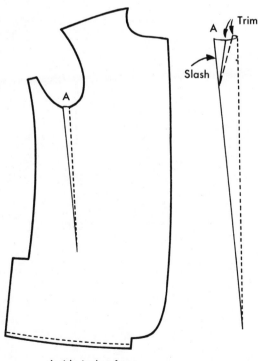

Inside jacket front

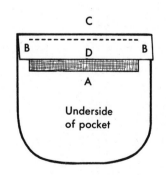

Underside of pocket

Inside the right front patch pocket, a little inside pocket may be made for keys or change!

Cut a piece of lining as indicated.

With right sides together, fold in half on lengthwise grain, and stitch ¼-inch side seams. Turn and press.

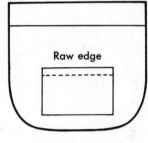

Pocket lining

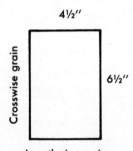

4½"

Crosswise grain

6½"

Lengthwise grain

Inside

Outside of
inner pocket

Stitch together raw edges ¼ inch from edge.

Stitch raw edge to patch pocket lining.

Turn up pocket and press. Stitch sides to patch pocket lining close to edge and diagonally at top for reinforcement.

Stitch together pocket piece and lining *precisely* ¼ inch from raw edges. Sew on pockets as directed in photographs on page 177, *BMCC*.

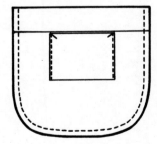

The second jacket photographed on page 184 has flap pockets instead of patch pockets at the bottom of the jacket.

They were made exactly like the directions on pages 172–174, *BMCC*, except that the lengthwise folded strip across the top was sewn to the flap before the flap was applied to the pocket piece.

Using automatic hem gauge, turn up hem of jacket 1½ inches and press.

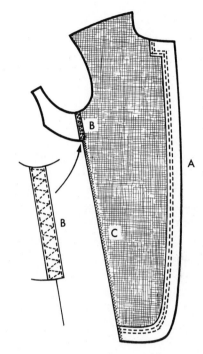

Front interfacing

### Jacket front interfacing unit

Match outer edge of the muslin strip with the outer edge of hair canvas (A). Place muslin strip on opposite side of hair canvas from center front and buttonhole markings.

Stitch muslin to hair canvas ⅞ inch from edge; stitch again near inside edge of muslin strip for reinforcement; press if necessary.

Butt edges of muslin and hair canvas interfacing at B and apply a piece of seam tape. Stitch at both edges of tape and zigzag back and forth to keep flat the butt edges of interfacing.

At C, use zigzag stitch on edge of hair canvas to control the off grain edge, or a staystitch ¼ inch from edge may be used.

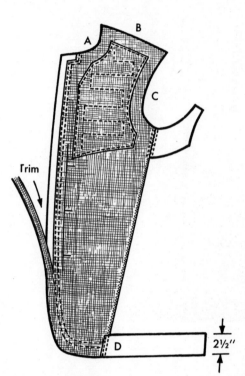

Trim away hair canvas to first row of stitching ⅞ inch from edge.

Place reinforcement piece on opposite side of interfacing from muslin strip. It will be on the same side as the center front and buttonhole markings. Reinforcement piece will be ⅞ inch from A, B, and C edges. Stitch around this section ¼ inch from all edges. Quilt a design at machine on true grain of section for added strength. If Pelomite is used, just press in place with hot iron.

Overlap bias muslin (cut 2½ inches wide) on hair canvas interfacing for ¼ inch (D). Stitch at edge of muslin and hair canvas to hold securely.

Place interfacing to underside of jacket front, muslin strip facing jacket. At A, cut away interfacing diagonally at corner ¼ inch beyond seamline to eliminate bulk.

Staystitch interfacing to jacket in direction shown just outside seamline. On front edge B, staystitch exactly on seamline up to center front line.

Stitch bias muslin in place at C about ¼ inch from lower edge of muslin. Stitching will be about ¼ inch from hem line. Muslin extends to raw edge of jacket side front (D).

In contrasting thread, baste-stitch center front and crosswise lines for buttonholes from interfacing through to outside of garment. Baste-stitch the crosswise lines before doing the lengthwise ones.

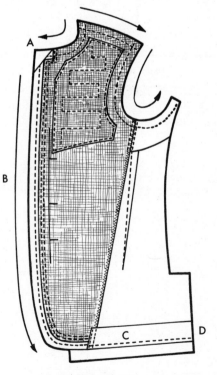

Jacket front

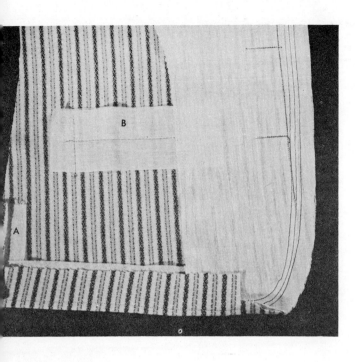

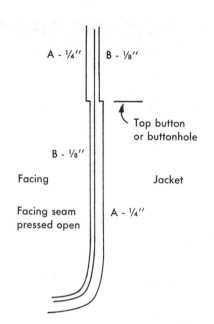

↙ Top button
or buttonhole

B - ⅛″

Facing            Jacket

Facing seam    A - ¼″
pressed open

In this lightweight jacket, just as you learned to do with the back unit, a straight strip of muslin is stitched in place at A to support the side pleat.

Flap pockets are always reinforced with a lengthwise muslin strip (B).

### Front facing unit

Staystitch neck (A) and inside (B) edges of facing on seamline. Staystitch lower edge (C) ¼ inch from edge for a distance of 2½ inches from bottom up.

Right sides together, place facing on jacket front, keying all edges with perfection.

With interfacing side up, stitch facings to jacket from lower edge of facing to center front line. Sew through staystitching on seamline and *favor* facings above markings for top buttonhole and button. Use short stitches for ½ inch on either side of corner.

At neckline, snip facing and jacket to seamline at center front.

Trim away muslin strip to seamline and press open facing seam on edge presser.

Stagger facing seam in trimming. The upper seam (A) is trimmed down to ¼ inch and the under seam (B) to ⅛ inch. At the top buttonhole and button, the ¼-inch seam will change to ⅛ inch, and the ⅛-inch seam to ¼ inch, because the facing reverses and becomes the topside. Trim away seam allowance in corner to within a few threads of seamline.

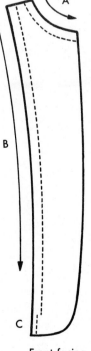

Front facing

Turn facing to inside and set the edge, pressing with underside *on top*. From the top buttonhole and button coming down, the underside will be the facing. From the top buttonhole and button, going up to the center front, the underside will be the garment.

After the edge has been set in pressing, turn and have jacket right side up. Press again and flatten facings, pockets, and hem with pounding block. Flatten lower edge of jacket back, also.

This photograph shows the finished front facing unit at the neckline.

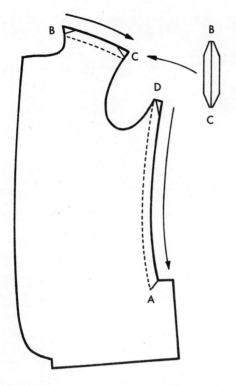

## Jacket unit

Stitch shoulder and side seams in direction shown. Clip diagonally ⅝ inch at A for pleat extension. Press open seams in the same direction they were stitched.

Leave interfacing in shoulder seam, but trim out of side seam near seamline. At B, C, and D, beginning 1¼ inches from edge, trim seam away diagonally to ⅛ inch to eliminate bulk at seamline.

## Collar unit

Staystitch with a longer stitch the top collar ⅝ inch from the edge in contrasting thread. At A and B edges, turn back seam allowance on staystitching, and press with perfection. At C corners, cut away bulk of seam, and whip raw edges together on a diagonal line.

The under collar is cut of lightweight felt, hard flannel, or other similar fabric; the interfacing has been cut of hair canvas and on the bias, as was the under collar. Staystitch ¾ inch from A, B, and D edges. Join center seam on seamline, trim interfacing away to seamline, press open seam, and topstitch both sides of seamline. Trim away under collar seam to topstitching.

Mark a quilting pattern on true grain of hair canvas for under collar.

Stitch quilting pattern at machine through felt and hair canvas. Trim hair canvas up to staystitching ¾ inch from edge at all outside edges, and trim felt ⅝ inch from edge.

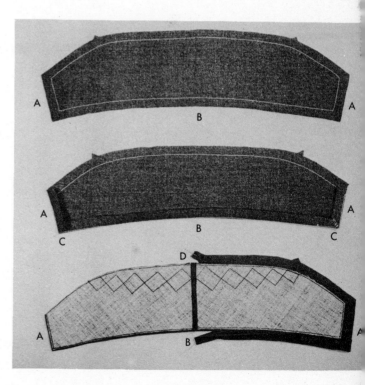

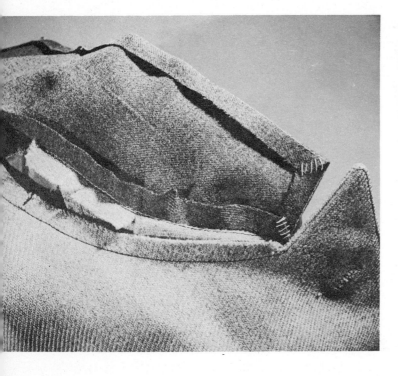

Sew top collar to front facings from center front to ⅝ inch from edge of facings at shoulder seam. Keep facing side up and sew through staystitching on seamline. Press open seam. Trim facing seam to ¼ inch and top collar seam to ⅜ inch as far up as shoulder seam of facings. By hand, loosely stitch front neckline edges of jacket to top collar seam.

Whipstitch the under collar to the top collar. Remove staystitching in contrasting thread from the top collar. The top collar is still free across the back from one edge of the front facing to the other.

Press the collar into a sharp crease at the fold line. It should fit the shirt collar with perfection. Use a cushion to shape the collar, and shrink, mold, and press the fold line. The crease extends ½ inch below the seamline of the collar into the lapel.

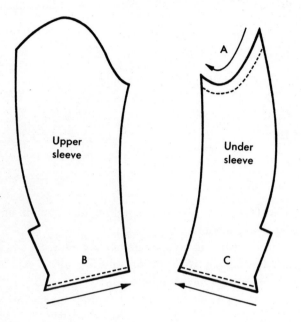

Upper sleeve

Under sleeve

A

B

C

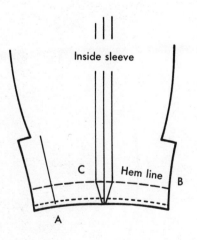

Inside sleeve

C    Hem line    B

A

### Sleeve unit

Staystitch A edge on seamline and B and C ¼ inch from edges in direction shown.

Stitch sleeve seam (D) in direction shown. The grain on this sleeve is such that the seam should be stitched from the bottom up. Press open seam, and at E, beginning 1¼ inches from edge, trim seam away diagonally to ⅛ inch to eliminate bulk at seamline. Trim seam at F to ¼ inch for depth of hem (1½ inches).

Cut a piece of hair canvas on the bias 3½ inches wide and long enough to extend ¼ inch beyond the fold line at A and all the way out to the raw edge at B. It will extend ½ inch beyond hem line (1½ inches from lower edge) at C.

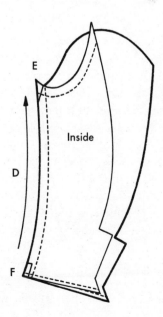

E

Inside

D

F

Stitch hair canvas in place ⅛ inch from edge at D, E, and F. Turn up and press hem of sleeve 1½ inches from lower edge, and turn back and press pleat extension on fold line.

Stitch second sleeve seam from armhole down, including pleat and hem, and using small stitches at corner G.

At G, clip diagonally to stitching in corner on under sleeve section.

At H, stitch all layers together ⅛ inch from edge, and bevel away with scissors all the under layers of fabric up to ⅛-inch stitching.

Press open sleeve seam and final-press pleat with perfection. At I, trim seam away diagonally.

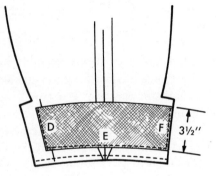

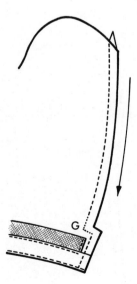

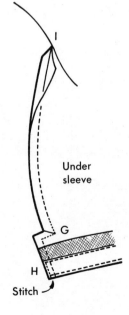

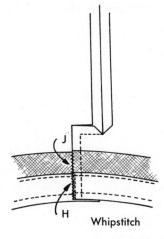

At H, whipstitch pleat edge to hem, only catching hem in stitching. Stitch down to bottom of hem and back up to top of it to hold edge securely. Whipstitch will have the appearance of a cross-stitch. At J, whipstitch pleat extension to hair canvas only. Catch-stitch hair canvas to second sleeve seam. See sketch with the lining on page 202.

Sew on 2, 3, or 4 buttons. They should start 1¼ inches from lower edge of sleeve and ½ inch from pleat line. They should never extend above the pleat line. It is not necessary to make a shank as you learned on pages 84–85, *BMCC*.

Draw buttonhole twist through the beeswax shown in the holder in the left of the photograph. This waxing prevents the thread from knotting and twisting. Used thread double in the needle, but separate it to make the chain stitch, as shown in the photograph. It is a false buttonhole and gives a nice, custom-looking touch.

Stitch sleeve seams of lining in same direction as jacket sleeve seams were stitched. Press open.

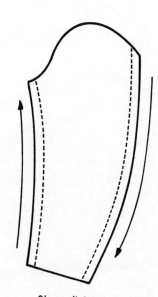

Sleeve lining

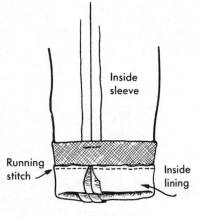

Inside
sleeve

Running
stitch

Inside
lining

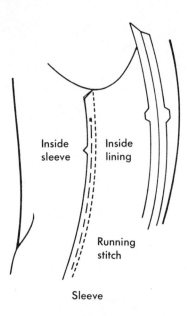

Inside
sleeve

Inside
lining

Running
stitch

Sleeve

Turn jacket sleeve wrong side out, and place right side of sleeve lining into right side of jacket sleeve. Bring raw edge of lining over to underside of sleeve to meet raw edge of hem. With a small running stitch ¼ inch from edge, sew lining to the top of the hem of the sleeve. The stitching must go through the hair canvas at the same time.

Bring the lining out of the jacket sleeve. With wrong sides together, catch seams of lining and jacket. Beginning about 2 inches below the armhole, attach one side of lining seam to corresponding side of sleeve seam with a single thread and a long, easy running stitch through the middle of the seam allowance. Fasten the thread about 3 inches above bias hair can-

vas. Make several back stitches at the beginning (even with a knot in the thread) and at the end of the stitching to secure the thread in fabric. Always favor the lining. Repeat for second seam.

Place hand in lining sleeve and turn on top of the jacket sleeve, turning the lining right side out. Press down excess lining at lower edge into what is known as a take-up tuck; this is necessary to prevent elbows from wearing through. See photograph on page 165, *BMCC*.

From one notch to the other, do off-grain stitching (page 157, *BMCC*) to prepare the sleeve cap to fit into the armhole.

Sew sleeve into armhole (page 157, *BMCC*). Do not trim any of the seam allowance or any interfacing from armhole until stitching in lining. For added strength underarm, you may stitch the seam a second time below the notches on the seamline.

To maintain a firm line on the cap of the sleeve, and to round out the ease, cut a piece of jacket fabric on true bias 3½ inches wide and 10 inches long. This length will vary with the size of the jacket. Fold and press lengthwise, bringing one raw edge within ½ inch of the other. With shorter raw edge (A) turned up, place folded edge of bias (B) ¼ inch from raw edge of armhole seam. Sew by hand as close as possible to the seamline of sleeve.

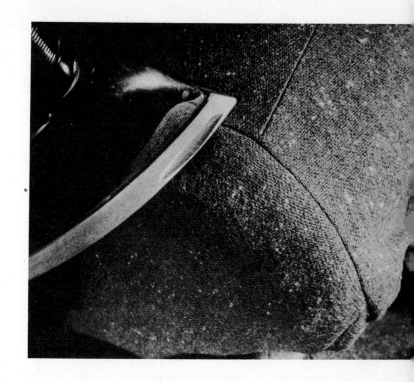

The armhole seam turns into the sleeve. From one notch to the other over the top of the sleeve, press seam flat on a cushion. Roll the iron out on top of the sleeve in pressing. Do not press seam underarm.

Men's garments have a smooth, round line over the cap of the sleeve, but women's garments have a soft, rolled one.

Match raw edges and key armhole of lining to armhole of sleeve at notches, underarm seam, and shoulder seam. With a loose running stitch, tack sleeve cap of lining to that of jacket, easing in lining fullness over cap. Below notches, take small running stitch close to seam. Trim seam (four thicknesses) to ¼ inch from notch to notch under the arm (see top photo, page 166, *BMCC*).

If shoulder shapes are needed to obtain a normal shoulder line, shoulder shapes are used in men's garments the same as women's. (Follow directions on pages 158–59, *BMCC*, for making them.) They should be sewn into the jacket at this time, before the body of the lining is attached. Key the shoulder seam of the shape to the shoulder seam of the jacket; also, key raw edge of shoulder shape at armhole to raw edge of armhole seam of jacket. With a running stitch, attach pad to jacket at shoulder and armhole seams. Catch edges of pad to muslin interfacing in back and hair canvas in front.

### Side pleats unit

At jacket side front, turn hem to outside on fold line, right sides together. Stitch ⅝-inch seam to top of hem (A). Press open seam, trim to ¼ inch, round off fabric in corner, turn right side out, and press.

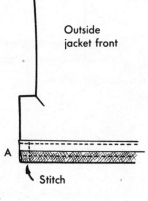

Outside
jacket front

A

Stitch

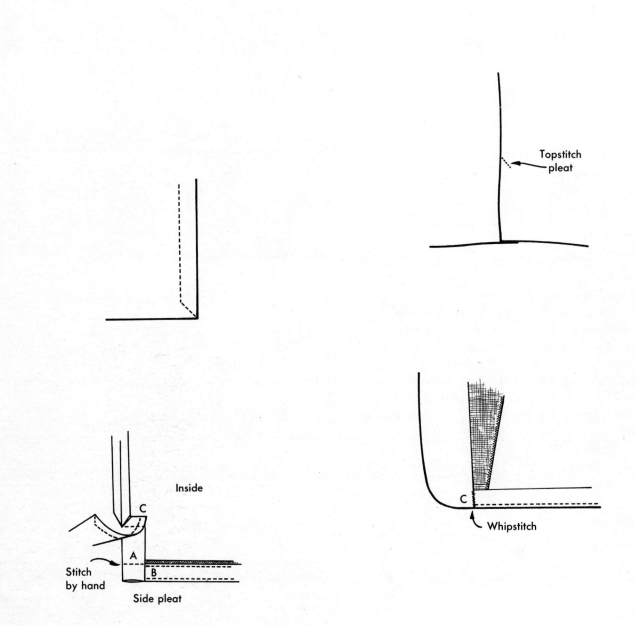

Inside

C

Stitch
by hand

A

B

Side pleat

Topstitch
pleat

C

Whipstitch

Topstitch ¼ inch from edge, going diagonally at lower corner.

At jacket side back, stitch facing by hand at A to hem only. Whipstitch B the same as pleat extension on sleeve. Lap raw edges of front and back pleat extensions to meet at C, and stitch together on machine.

Topstitch pleat at slight angle for ¾ inch from pleat edge. The two pleats at the sides of a jacket are preferred over one at the center back, and most jackets have two instead of one.

Finish lower edge of front facing (C) the same as pleat extension on the sleeve.

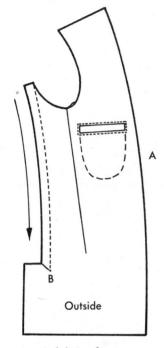

Left lining front

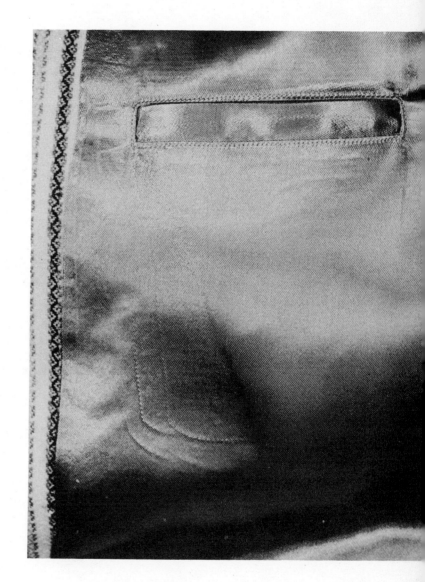

## Lining unit

On left side of lining front, and beginning 1¼ inches from front raw edge (A), make modified welt pocket (pages 114–115, *BMCC*). Sew side seams of lining fronts and back in direction shown to marking for pleat extension. On lining fronts, clip diagonally to stitching at pleat opening (B).

This photograph shows the modified welt pocket in the completed front lining. Press open seams. Sew underarm darts and press toward front; jacket darts have been pressed toward back. Staystitch back neckline on seamline.

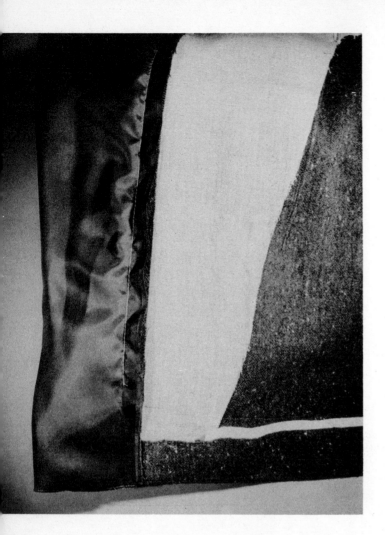

The center back pleat is stitched the same as the woman's jacket on page 165, *BMCC*. Catch-stitch in position at the waistline.

Place right side of lining to right side of front facings, and with facing side up, sew lining to both facing edges with a ⅝-inch seam to 2 inches above top of jacket hem. Stitch one thread inside staystitching on facings on seamline. Use the longest stitch at the machine unless it puckers. If so, shorten stitch slightly.

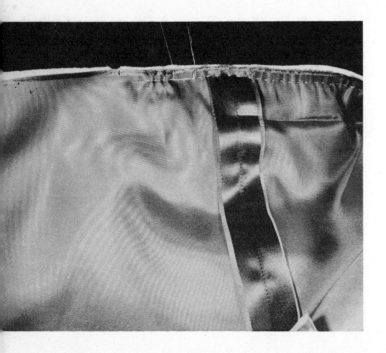

Bring the raw edge of the lining over to the underside of jacket hem to meet raw edge of hem (same as sleeves were done). With a small running stitch ¼ inch from raw edge, sew lining to hem, catching front interfacing and center back seam.

Turn lining to inside of jacket and with wrong sides together, beginning 2 inches below armhole, catch underarm seams of lining and jacket, same as sleeve lining seams (page 202).

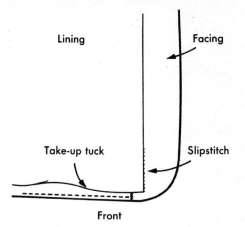

Press down excess lining at lower edge of front facings. This is known as a take-up tuck, and is necessary for longer wear on the lining. Complete lower edge of front facings with slipstitching and include take-up tuck to hold in place. Press lining flat at front facings.

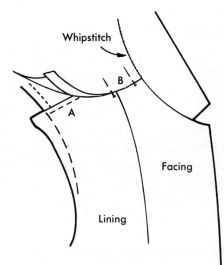

Key raw shoulder edge of lining front to raw edge of back half of jacket shoulder seam (A). Attach with an easy running stitch.

Turn under seam allowance on the shoulders of lining back and lap ⅝ inch over lining front; pin in place (B).

Match neck edge of lining to seamline of jacket, and attach with an easy running stitch (A). Turn under top collar ⅝ inch and bring ⅝ inch over lining back (B); pin in place. Whipstitch top collar and back shoulders in place. Make small stitches with heavy-duty thread or buttonhole twist.

Whipstitch lining in place around the armholes the same as a woman's garment (bottom of page 167, BMCC).

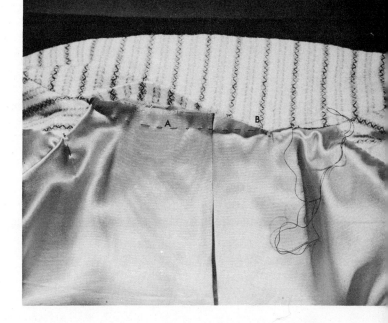

This technique for finishing the body of the lining over the sleeve lining is not the usual method found in ready-to-wear. However, it gives longer wear; there is no pull on the stitches; it is easier to do, and is a repeat performance of the method in women's tailoring.

To complete side pleats, turn in lining front to ¼ inch from finished edge of pleat (A); slipstitch. Finish take-up tuck same as front edge.

Slash into back lining at an angle until back lining can be turned under to meet edge of front pleat with perfection (B). Cut away excess lining. Turn under and slipstitch top and side to complete pleat extension. Finish take-up tuck same as front edge. Press take-up tuck in place at entire lower edge of jacket.

Make keyhole buttonholes in left front and regular buttonhole on left lapel, if desired. They may be done with a buttonhole attachment, and then embroidered over that by hand with a buttonhole stitch, using buttonhole twist. Sew on buttons with a good shank on right front (pages 84–85, *BMCC*).

Remove baste-stitching at pleat in center back of lining. Press lining at edge of top collar, but not across shoulders or around armholes. If the outer fabric has become wrinkled from the handling as the lining was being attached, some light final-pressing may again be necessary on the jacket.

# Chapter 14

# Trimming details for the quality look

The chapter in our first book on trimming details was so well received that we are adding one to this book, also.

The principle in the Bishop method has been that you work toward learning to express yourself by adding a trimming detail when it will help to obtain a quality look. Do not be a slave to a pattern, but add the right personal touch to your garment, as a designer will do.

In seeking the right trimming detail, you will often get a hint from either the fabric or the style of the garment. Many times you will get an idea from a fabric, especially a design idea, before ever cutting it out. Other times an idea will come to you as you work on the garment; or playing with scraps may give you an idea in seeking the right detail for the quality look.

However, as much as we have stressed trimming details in these two chapters, we would also like to emphasize that not every garment needs trimming. The lines of the garment may be impressive, or the fabric may be individual. The garment may then stand completely on its own.

1. The rose was made following the directions with the next photograph. The leaves were made on the bias, as shown on page 223. Instead of a buttonhole, the jacket is fastened with a silk-covered snap, sewn on the facing under the rose.

The rose would be attractive many other places— at the waistline, near the hemline in clusters, grouped at a neckline, etc.

## Trimming details for the quality look

Embroider French knots in a square of fabric (A). Cut a circle of cardboard, place a mound of cotton on top, and cut square (A) to fit around circle; stitch by hand. The cotton gives a raised effect in the center. Fold true bias (B) right sides out, and stitch near raw edges. Lap small pieces of bias and tack around circle shown at C. The last piece of bias (D) is sewn from the underside; then, it rolls up to cover raw edges of circle and bias.

**2.** When a suit or dress is completed, these bows may be added. The half of the bow at A is placed at the edge of the buttonhole. The other half of the bow at B is placed on the other side just at the edge of the right front of the jacket. See directions with the sketch that follows.

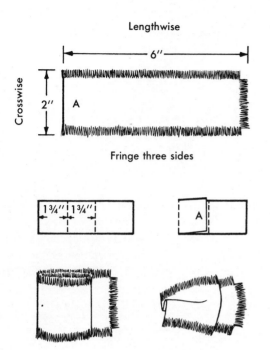

Lengthwise

Crosswise

6″

2″

A

Fringe three sides

1¾″ 1¾″

A

Tear or pull threads and cut a lengthwise piece of fabric 2 inches by 6 inches for each half of the bow. Fringe all edges except A, or make double in finer fabric, such as silk linen.

Make a double turn at A edge for a depth of 1¾ inches each time. Fold a pleat at inside edge of bow and invisibly stitch to hold in place. Press this edge only. Hand sew bow in place on garment.

**3.** These flower buttons may be the real touch of drama on a jacket or dress. Made of self-fabric, they are sewn on the jacket, and silk-covered snaps (page 214) are used to fasten the garment on the underside. However, the buttons could be used equally well with buttonholes. To make these buttons, see directions with the next photograph.

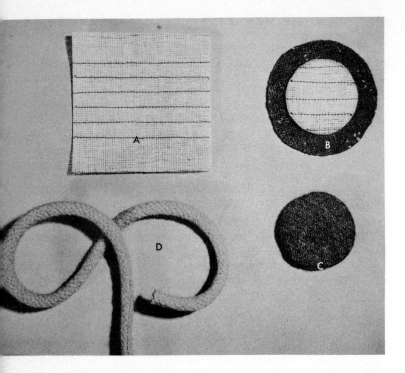

Sew together several layers of crinoline or buckram (A). Then, cut circle desired size, and place in the middle of a self-fabric circle (B). Run a baste-stitch around fabric circle ¼ inch from edge, and draw up basting; fasten circle neatly with hand stitches (C). Make bias strip (D) as you learned on page 193, *The Bishop Method of Clothing Construction.*\* Press open on wooden dowel, shown at A in next photograph. Beginning at center, on the smooth side of the circle, fasten an end of the bias strip. Make a loop and tack it to the circle; continue until the circle is covered with the loops.

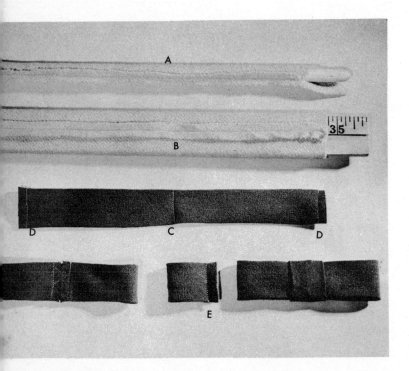

4. Many times, there is nothing that will add so much to a dress as a pretty bow placed with an artist's touch here or there.

The A was just added to the photograph to show how narrow bias can be pressed open on a dowel. The wider bias used for the bow is shown at B, being pressed open on a yardstick. The seam will be placed to the center of the underside.

The row of stitching at C identifies the center for the bow to which the raw edges at D are placed and stitched flat.

The center of the bow is also seamed (E), pressed open, turned right side out, and slid in place at the center of the bow.

These basic techniques will help you in making any bow.

\*Referred to hereafter as *BMCC*.

**5.** The pocket flaps are the important detail on this jacket; so the buttons and buttonholes are few in number, and plain, covered buttons were used.

The fringes on A flaps are a different color from the fringes on B flaps, because the A ones were made from a lengthwise strip, while the B ones were made from a crosswise strip. At the lower edges (C), the fabric was folded, and the threads were pulled from the top layer only to form the fringed look. That way, the fringe will not fray at the lower edge.

**6.** This detail would be smart-looking on the front of dresses and blouses as well as suits. Silk snaps were used to fasten this jacket on the underside, but buttonholes could easily be made under the flaps.

After these square flaps were fringed, two were sewn together by hand near the inside edge of the fringe to give each one more character than a single layer of wool. Then, the flaps were tacked to the jacket with invisible hand stitches at the upper corners.

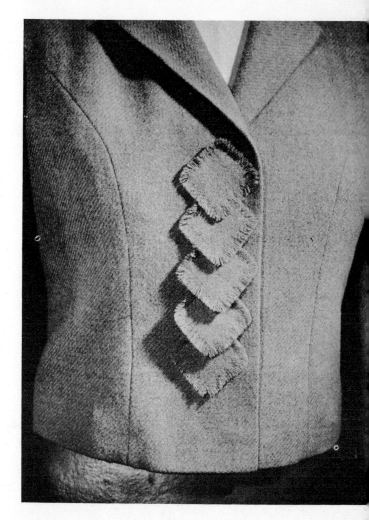

## Trimming details for the quality look

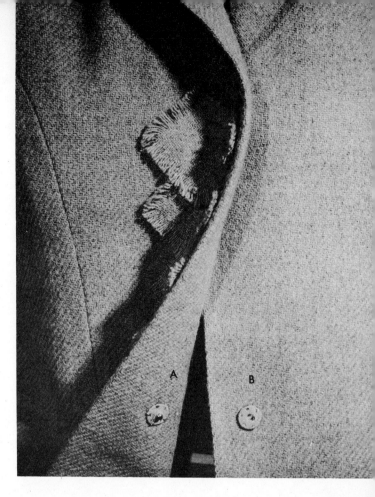

**7.** Covering snaps (A and B) with matching lining fabric is an important step toward having quality looking clothes. Use snaps approximately ½ inch in diameter. Follow directions below.

The circle (A) is usually the size of a small spool of thread. Punch a hole with a stiletto and place lining over snap (B). Sew around circle of lining; draw up thread and fasten neatly on underside of snap.

Place second circle over second half of snap. Close the snap, and while the snap is together, sew around second circle of lining; draw up thread and fasten neatly on underside of snap.

C and D show the completed snap before it is sewn on the garment. Feel with the needle for holes in snaps, and be certain to sew snap to garment through holes of snap.

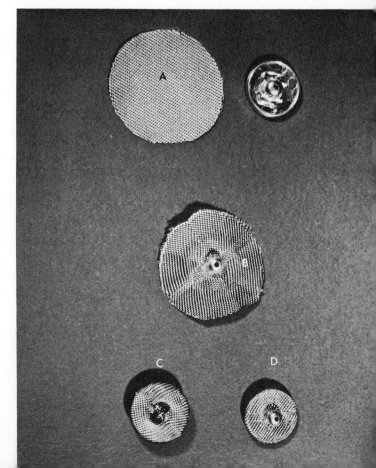

**8.** Buttons with fringe of matching fabric will be a conversation piece on a suit. The ones on A jacket are used with buttonholes, but the ones on B jacket have the silk covered snaps on the underside. It would be overpowering to have three of this detail on a short jacket—two are better in design. One should be placed at the bustline.

Two circles of folded fringe are sewn under the covered button. You can see that the fringe in A, which is crosswise, would be a different color from B, which is lengthwise of the fabric. Use the color that is most flattering to your fabric.

Fold and press fringe and sew through seam allowance with a running stitch; draw fringe to form a circle; press flat. The second circle is made smaller than the first.

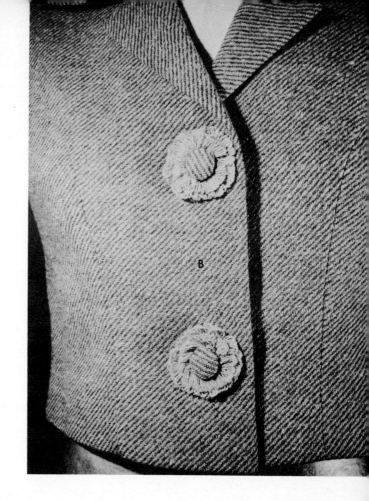

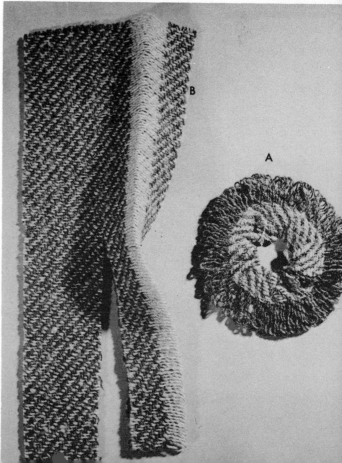

**9.** When a dress, blouse, jacket, or coat is completed, these interesting tabs can be slipped through the buttonhole, and hand sewn in place. They are made double, and slashed on the underside (page 121, *BMCC*) to turn and press.

We are showing the pattern for the tabs without any seam allowance. However, they may be made smaller, depending upon the type of garment and the number used.

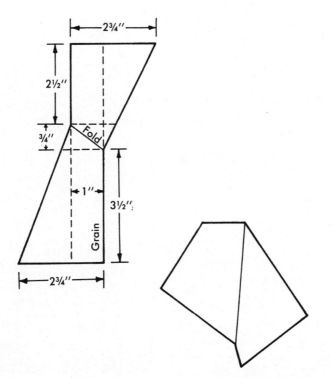

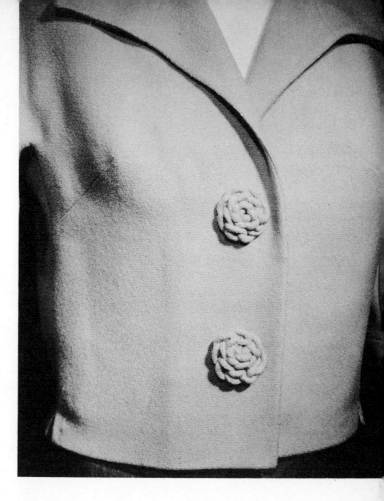

**10.** These crocheted buttons will add charm to any tailored garment. They are sewn on this jacket, and silk snaps were used on the underside for fastening. The pattern is the same as the suit on page 213.

To make the crocheted buttons, take the end of the bias and form a loop; stitch by hand. Then, make six single crochet stitches; join to first permanent loop. Continue with double crochet stitches around the first six single ones. Pull bias through last stitch and stitch by hand on underside. Pull starting loop up to make center of button (A).

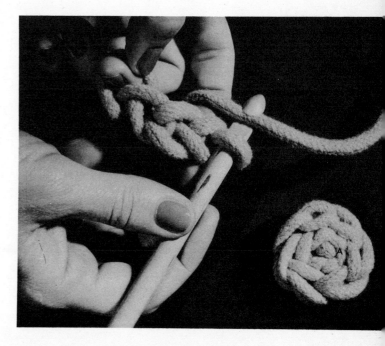

**11.** These tabs will be unusual used on the lower edge of a jacket, bolero, toppette, or skirt. They can also be sewn into the seam of a collar. Do not make them in heavy fabric.

Fold raw edges to meet in center of tab (A). Then, fold tab in half and stitch ends together (B). The tabs are ready to insert into a seam or on an edge with a facing.

**12.** These tulips give a designer's touch and can be used over the buttonhole on a suit of linen, silk linen, lightweight woolen, etc. A machine buttonhole is all that is necessary, because it will not show. The directions are given with the next photograph.

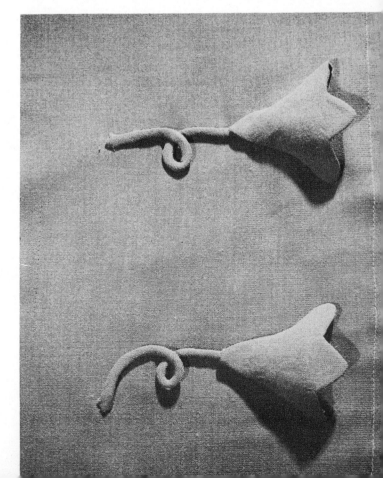

Cut a piece of Pelomite the desired size of finished tulip (A). Press on a square of fabric so that the lengthwise grain of fabric goes from top to bottom of tulip (B). Place a second square below the first one (C) on identical lengthwise grain.

Stitch around edge of Pelomite with smallest stitch machine will make. Trim square B to ⅛-inch seam allowance. Clip to stitching at points of tulip (D and D). Press seam up. Then, trim under-square C to ⅛-inch seam allowance and clip to stitching at points of tulip (D and D). In center of tulip, make a slash on underside to turn right side out and press.

When tacking tulip to garment, allow for sufficient space to cover button.

Bias (page 193, *BMCC*) is slipped under lower edge of tulip when being invisibly sewn to garment.

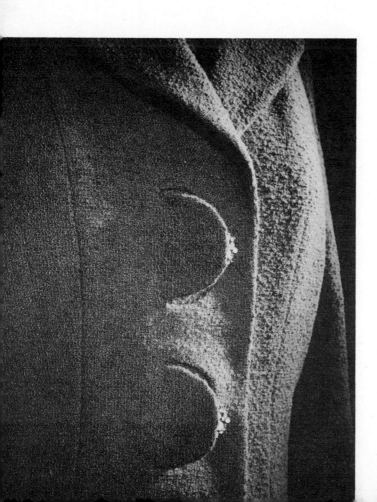

**13.** The half-circle button closure is extremely smart on a jacket with jeweled or special-interest buttons.

## Trimming details for the quality look

Mark position of half-circle opening on underside of garment. Cut a facing patch on identical grain of jacket, and place on jacket, right sides together. Using a small stitch, sew a few threads either side of the half-circle marking.

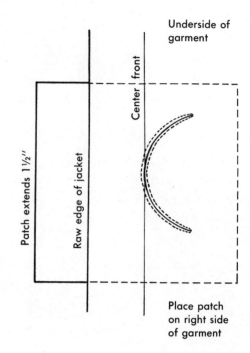

Cut through center of stitching. Pull facing patch through slit to underside of garment. Press entire area. Next, fold facing patch back on half circle at fold line marked on the sketch. Press carefully on grain. Stitch suitable interfacing or underlining for garment on underside.

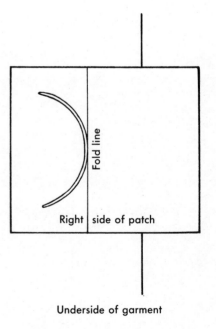

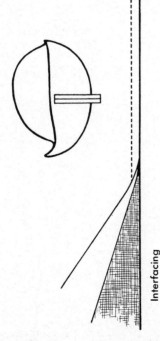

Make a tailored buttonhole through facing patch and interfacing. Proceed with completing jacket by putting on facings. Use a button with special interest.

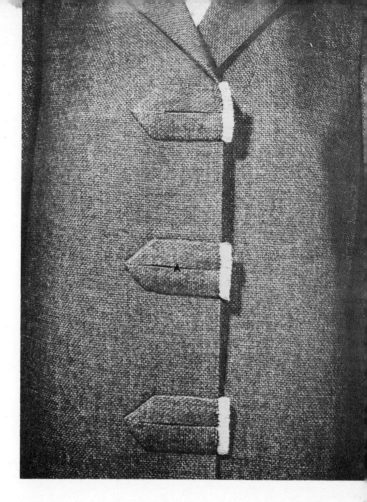

**14.** This intriguing detail could be used on any garment.   The straps may cover the buttons and button-holes, and you would reach inside at the opening (A) to open and close the garment.

However, if it is desired to display the buttons, they may be brought on top of the strap, as in this photograph.

To make straps, see directions with sketch on next page.

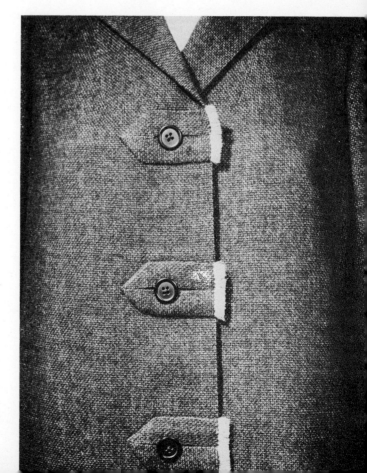

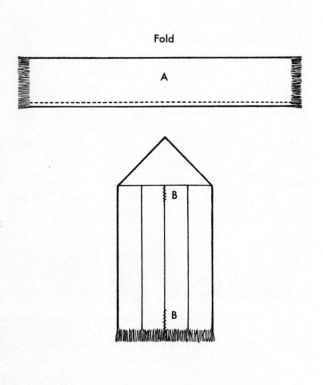

To make straps, fold a lengthwise strip of fabric in half (A), right sides together, and make a ¼-inch seam. Fringe both ends. Press seam open on dowel (page 212), turn strap right side out, and press flat with seam in the center on the underside.

Press to form a perfect mitered corner. Invisibly stitch strap together at B and B. Slipstitch in place on garment.

**15.** Starting at both shoulders, this versatile detail makes an attractive, self-trim on this peau de soie dinner dress. Note how it was used to give a finish at the waistline and on the lower edge of the sleeves. The next photograph describes the steps in making it.

To have a rounded and finished end, as shown at A in the photograph, fold true bias (B), right sides together. Then, fold lengthwise line in half, and stitch a mitered line, ending ¼ inch from lower fold (C).

Trim away excess fabric at miter, and pull two bias strips right side out.

Stitch the four raw edges together (D) in a narrow seam, holding true bias with perfection at fold line. In some fabrics, you may pull slightly as you stitch.

**16.** Two pockets were used for the trim on this dress. The leaves were made lengthwise following the directions on the bottom of page 121, *BMCC*. They were folded into a small tuck at the top to give a full look and were sewn by hand to the pockets.

The two pieces of bias that are tied at the waistline are just long enough to extend into the upper pocket.

The four pieces of bias below the pocket are sewn in place under the lower pocket and lower edge of skirt.

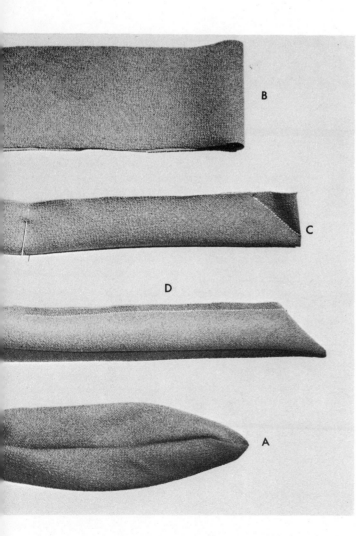

223

**17.** A basic dress gives you a very wide choice of detail. Large pockets continue in the fashion picture; these double ones are made on lengthwise grain. The fringe is double, and was made in the body of the fabric before the hem was turned. The pockets are placed and tacked over the belt.

**18.** Sequins with small crystal beads sewn in the center of them make a timeless detail and attractive outline for a print. They were used on the collar and bow of this dinner dress. The color of the sequins should accent the most becoming color in the print.

The finish on the bottom of the sleeve is the simulated cuff shown on page 76, *BMCC*.

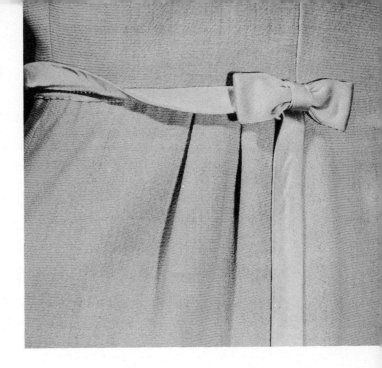

**19.** A folded piece of bias is stitched on the waistline seam of this dress and then turned down. It not only makes an attractive finish, but is more slenderizing and more flattering on many figures than a belt.

**20.** (*bottom left*) A bias bow can be placed in many attractive ways on a garment for a quality looking detail.

The bias finish at the waistline is the same as that on the previous dress.

**21.** (*bottom right*) Appliqués in an unusual design can add much quality to a basic dress.

Cut design from Pelomite and press on lengthwise piece of fabric. Trim fabric to within ¼ inch of the edge of the Pelomite, clip into corners, and press seam to underside.

Place appliqué on center dress front a little higher above than below the belt-line; pin in place. Invisibly slip-stitch appliqué to dress. For a wool or dull crepe dress, make design of matching satin or velvet. A shade darker or lighter than the dress color is also attractive. Self fabric is always a smart choice, too.

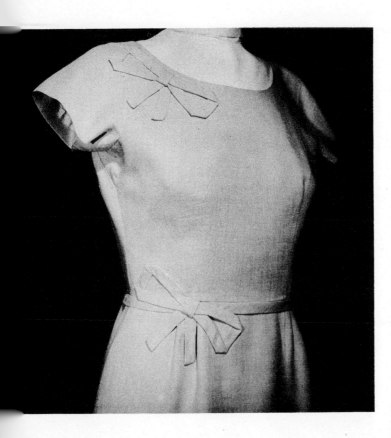

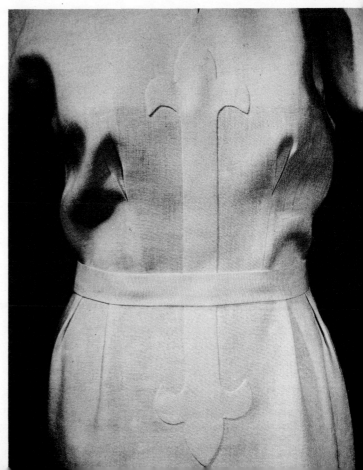

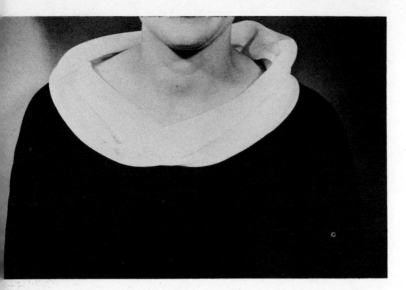

**22.** The "smoke ring" gives an added soft touch to a plain bateau or scoop neckline. This one was made of silk chiffon, but other fabric that has a draping quality (such as Paisley silk print) is desirable, too. The directions are given with the following sketches.

Cut a piece of fabric on true bias, 31 inches long and 14½ inches deep. Ends A are straight of grain.

Fold fabric lengthwise, right sides together, and sew a ¼-inch seam, beginning and ending ¼ inch from each end (B). Press open seam. Turn right side out. Place together right sides of straight-of-grain edges (A in first sketch) and sew a ¼-inch seam. Press open seam, and pull to inside.

Right sides together, sew remaining bias edges together, leaving a small opening to turn right side out.

Turn in raw edges and slipstitch opening by hand. Press smoke ring. If ring is too large for neckline, shorten length several inches.

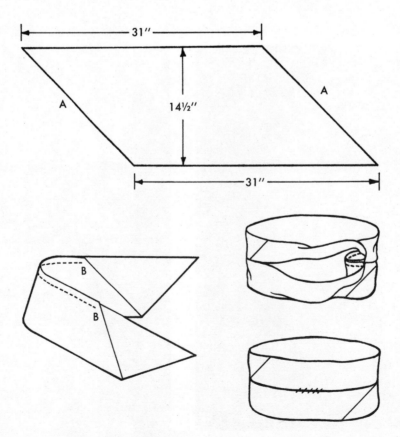

**23.** The trim on this dress is available by the yard and comes in many colors. It is applied to the dress by hand. Here the same triangular design was used on the front and back of the dress. Note how it was cut and arranged to form the point at the center front. On the belt, a small piece was used to add a finish to the folded ends of the bias belt. The belt fastens at the side with two hooks and eyes.

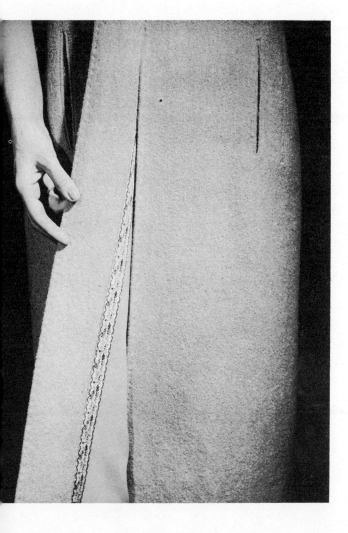

**24.** A different and expensive touch on a suit or coat is to sew pretty braid at the edge of the facing and lining.

**25.** The most desirable way to put a velvet or velveteen collar on a tailored garment is to complete the garment, and then add the extra collar. This way the velvet collar can be removed when it gets worn-looking.

Baste-stitch the collar the desired width from the edge that the velvet collar will begin. Cut the velvet collar from the top collar pattern but on the bias, cutting away the difference in the size of the top collar and the ⅝-inch seam allowance. Allow a ¼-inch seam on the velvet collar, and staystitch that distance from the edge. Turn under seam allowance on staystitching and press to perfection. Invisibly slipstitch the velvet collar to the top collar, going through stitching on top collar to give it a set-in look.

**26.** Gingham embroidery is fun and popular. Use it on a blouse, pocket of a shirt, or bodice of a child's dress; or use it as groups of one design to make a border around the skirt. Gingham with ⅛-inch checks is recommended, and the designs are worked in cross stitches and straight stitches. When making cross stitches, top strands should all point in the same direction.

Use three strands of six-strand floss, and starting at A in a white square, follow chart to make design. We suggest that the first motif be embroidered in white, the dog in blue, and the flowers in green, red, blue, and orange, as indicated.

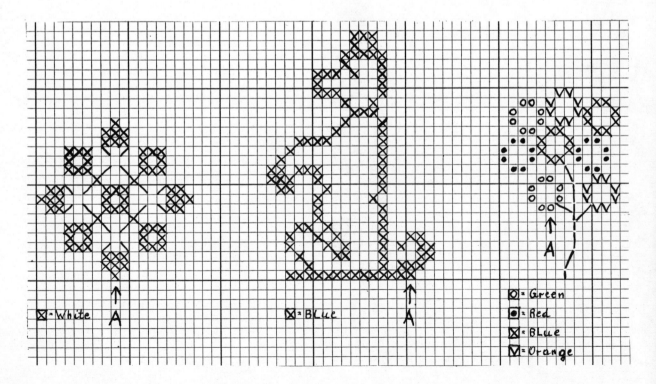

**anchor-stitch:** stitching about ½ inch long at a given area for reinforcement. Use a short zigzag stitch at machine. If you do not have a zigzag machine, stitch back and forth several times for about ½ inch.

**bar tack:** reinforcement by stitching at an area of a garment that gets a lot of pull or strain.

**baste-stitch:** the longest machine stitch, 6 to 8 per inch. With contrasting thread, it is used for basting and for marking location lines for buttonholes, pockets, and center fronts. With matching thread, it is used for control of ease on sleeve caps.

**beveling edges:** trimming away the seam allowance inside faced edges by using a slanted angle with the scissors to alleviate bulk in heavy fabric.

**bias:** a diagonal slant in a fabric that does not exactly follow the lengthwise or crosswise grain. True bias makes a 45° angle across the lengthwise and crosswise grain, and has greater stretch and less raveling than any other cut edge.

**binding:** enclosing both sides of an edge with a strip of fabric.

**box plait:** finished vertical strip that is sometimes used on the front of shirts. All men's dress shirts have this.

**catch-stitch:** a hand stitch, taken from right to left at a lower boundary and then at an upper boundary, which forms a triangular design.

**clean finishing:** turning a raw edge to the inside for ⅛ or ¼ inch on a line of staystitching, and then stitching on the edge. Clean finishing is used to finish the raw edges of facings and hems.

**dart:** a fold of fabric stitched to give shape to a garment, wide at one end and tapering to a point at the other end.

**directional staystitching:** a line of regulation machine stitching with matching thread, stitched through a single piece of fabric and placed just outside the seamline unless otherwise stated. It holds the grain threads in position, prevents fabric from stretching, and maintains the pattern line.

**directional stitching:** stitching seams in the correct direction of the grain to hold the grain threads in position, to prevent the fabric from stretching, and to maintain the pattern line.

**drum:** lining for a skirt. It is made with a firm fabric and gives support to the skirt. It is not sewn into the seams.

**ease:** working in extra fabric when stitching to a shorter piece of fabric without having gathers or small tucks.

**facing:** a piece of fabric cut on grain identical to the garment's, which is used to finish edges, such as necklines and sleeves. Facing may be finished to either the right side or the wrong side of the garment.

**favor:** ease fabric slightly on front facings above markings for top button and buttonhole.

**grain:** fabric is woven with the threads interlaced lengthwise and crosswise. The crosswise threads from selvage to selvage form the crosswise grain; the lengthwise threads running parallel with the selvage form the lengthwise grain. When the lengthwise and crosswise threads lie at perfect right angles, the fabric is grain perfect.

**hand picking:** a running stitch that pricks through the interfacing and penetrates into fabrics with depth. It is used as an edge finish in tailoring. For a zipper the technique is different and is shown on page 41.

**interfacing:** the fabric that is placed between the inside and the outside of the garment sections, such as in collars and cuffs. Interfacing gives body and better form to the appearance of the finished garment.

**lockstitching:** knotting the machine thread at the beginning and at the end of a line of stitching by releasing pressure on the presser foot, and stitching several times in the same stitch. Lockstitching eliminates the time and nuisance of tying threads, and the time and motion of using a reverse stitch.

**miter:** the angle formed when the excess fabric has been removed from a corner by a diagonal seam.

**notches:** the V-shaped markings on the edge of a pattern to indicate where corresponding pattern pieces are to be joined.

**overcast:** long, loose stitches over the raw edges of a seam to prevent raveling.

**regulation, or permanent, stitch:** the permanent stitch that is placed in a garment, 12 to 15 per inch, with matching thread. The number of stitches will vary with the type of fabric; a firm, fine fabric will take a shorter stitch than will a thick, heavy fabric.

**running stitch:** a hand stitch made by placing the needle in and out of the fabric in an even, straightforward manner.

**seam allowance:** the portion of a garment allowed for the seam, usually ⅝ inch.

**seamline:** the exact line where a seam is stitched.

**selvage:** the two lengthwise finished edges (parallel with the warp threads) on all woven fabric.

**shank:** the space between button and fabric, on all garments, to give room for the buttonhole side of the garment. It is made with thread unless the button has a metal shank.

short stitch: a shorter machine stitch, 18 to 20 per inch, used for reinforcement on comparatively limited areas, such as points of collars, underarm curves that must be clipped, and tailored buttonholes.

slipstitch: a concealed hand stitch that can be used only on an area with a folded edge. The needle is run along the fold of the hem for about ¼ inch; with a downward movement the garment is pricked; the needle is then brought out at the side of the fold. To continue slipstitching, the needle is placed back into the fold of the hem at about the same place, and the same procedure is repeated.

staystitching plus: manipulating the fabric with the machine stitch to force together the grain threads. It is an easy method for gaining control of ease.

stiletto: a pointed instrument that is used for making eyelet holes, etc.

topstitching: stitching a seam or edge on the right side of a garment with one or more rows of stitching.

tuck: a fold of fabric stitched to give shape to a garment.

underlay: section of fabric attached to drum or underlining of skirt back, forming the underpart of a pleat.

underlining: a second piece of fabric, cut from the same pattern pieces and on the same grain as the garment, staystitched to the outside fabric, and treated as one piece with the outside fabric for further construction. It gives a sculptured and quality look to a garment. When a dress is underlined, interfacings are usually not necessary.

understitching: a row of machine stitching placed close to the edge of any facing, which catches the two trimmed seams to the facing. It keeps the facing to the underside, and sharpens the seam edge.

unit construction: assembling the sections of a garment that make a unit, and completing all stitching and pressing before each unit is joined to another. This process involves less handling, improves organization of work, guarantees better quality-looking clothes, and enables shorter periods of time to be used to advantage.

whipstitch: a hand stitch that is used over a turned edge when sewing together two pieces of fabric.